LIN-MANUEL
MIRANDA

COMPOSER, ACTOR, AND
CREATOR OF *HAMILTON*

Kat Harrison

Enslow Publishing
101 W. 23rd Street
Suite 240
New York, NY 10011
USA
enslow.com

The author would like to thank her grandmother, for telling her it was okay to sing at the dinner table; her father, for teaching her what songs to sing; and her mother, for putting up with all of it.

Published in 2018 by Enslow Publishing, LLC.
101 W. 23rd Street, Suite 240, New York, NY 10011

Library of Congress Cataloging-in-Publication Data

Names: Harrison, Kat, 1987– author.
Title: Lin-Manuel Miranda : composer, actor, and creator of Hamilton / Kat Harrison.
Description: New York : Enslow Publishing, 2018. | Series: Influential lives | Includes bibliographical references and index. | Audience: Grades 6–12.
Identifiers: LCCN 2017003044 | ISBN 9780766085053 (library-bound)
Subjects: LCSH: Miranda, Lin-Manuel, 1980-—Juvenile literature. | Actors—United States—Biography—Juvenile literature. | Composers—United States—Biography—Juvenile literature. | Lyricists—United States—Biography—Juvenile literature.
Classification: LCC PN2287.M6446 H37 2017 | DDC 792.02/8092 [B] —dc23
LC record available at https://lccn.loc.gov/2017003044

Printed in the United States of America

Contents

CHAPTER ONE

A Star Is Born

· ·

Without a doubt, Lin-Manuel Miranda is the most famous Broadway star of the twenty-first century. Not only did he revolutionize Broadway theater but he has been able to cross over into film, television, music, and pop culture.

Before he turned thirty-seven, he had created the biggest Broadway hit in history, become one of the youngest people ever to receive the MacArthur "Genius" Grant, amassed a tremendous following on social media, been awarded several honorary degrees from top universities in the United States, and become one of the most recognizable names in the entertainment industry. The recipient of multiple Tony Awards, Grammys, and a Pulitzer Prize, Miranda is lauded as one of the brightest stars of his generation.

· · · · · · · · · · · · · · · · · · · ·

Lin-Manuel Miranda is best known for creating the wildly successful hip-hop musical *Hamilton*. But Miranda has lived a life full of music, theater, and politics.

A native New Yorker, Miranda has always been surrounded by a wide variety of influences. His family encouraged his love and enjoyment of music, but hoped he would become a lawyer, because not only was it a much more stable career but it also would allow the young Miranda to use his intellect. He is proud to be Puerto Rican and American and a New Yorker.

But Lin-Manuel was destined for the stage, not the courtroom. Over years of hard work absorbing and creating musical theater, he grew to become the biggest Broadway star of a generation. He not only re-created an interest in the Broadway musical but he brought it into the twenty-first century and made it "cool" again. After *Hamilton* premiered in 2015, the show was an immediate hit, selling out months in advance. Even after Miranda left his starring role to pursue other projects, the show remained sold out for another year.

It is clear, if nothing else, that Lin-Manuel Miranda will go down in history as making the founding fathers once again a part of American pop culture. He created an entirely new genre of Broadway musical, one that incorporates the modern sounds of music with a classic story. He has had the good fortune to have worked with some of his theater, film, and music idols, and has so many projects lined up, it's quite clear that Lin-Manuel Miranda isn't going anywhere anytime soon.

Growing Up Miranda

Lin-Manuel Miranda was born on January 16, 1980, in Washington Heights, one of the uppermost neighborhoods in Manhattan, New York City. His parents

Miranda grew up in a Puerto Rican family in the New York City neighborhood of Washington Heights, located in northern Manhattan. This upbringing would influence him for the rest of his life.

• •

are both Puerto Rican and had active careers in New York City. His mother, Luz, was a clinical psychologist, and his father, Luis A. Miranda Jr., was a Democratic Party consultant. Lin-Manuel was the younger of two children, with an older sister, Luz, named after her mother. His parents took the name "Lin-Manuel" from a poem about the Vietnam War, *Nana Roja Para Mi Hijo Lin Manuel*, written by Puerto Rican author José Manuel Torres Santiago.

The neighborhood of Washington Heights is mostly Latino, with residents hailing from the Dominican Republic, Cuba, and Puerto Rico. The Miranda family is Puerto Rican. Lin-Manuel and his sister spent a month out of every summer in Vega Alta, Puerto Rico. Miranda is fluent in Spanish and English, and very proud of his heritage.[1] The diversity of the Washington Heights neighborhood allowed Miranda to explore and celebrate his heritage. He heard salsa music coming from apartment windows, Spanish being spoken at home and in the streets, and the rhythmic pulse of New York City and its multicultural inhabitants.

Lin-Manuel began studying piano at a very young age. At home, he was surrounded by music. His parents played many cast albums from Broadway shows. His mother was a fan of classics such as *Camelot*, *A Chorus Line*, and *Les Miserables*. His father's favorite score was from *The Unsinkable Molly Brown*.[2] He also heard the works of Rodgers and Hammerstein, such as *Oklahoma* and *The Sound of Music*, and also *Chicago*, *West Side Story*, and *Carousel*. Because music was so important to the Miranda family, both children started learning the piano at a young age. By the time Lin-Manuel was in the second grade, he was known for his love of the attention he received from performing in front of a crowd. His first performances were rocky, but soon he had to be dragged from the stage.

Early Influences

He was exposed to early hip hop, Latin music such as salsa and merengue, classical, and rock music in Washington Heights. His school bus driver taught Lin-Manuel about hip-hop and rap, in particular Boogie Down Productions, Geto Boys, and the Sugarhill Gang.

The Sugarhill Gang (*left to right*: Michael 'Wonder Mike' Wright, Guy 'Master Gee' O'Brian, and Henry 'Big Bank' Jackson) were an early influence of Lin-Manuel Miranda's. They were also one of the first popular hip-hop groups.

• •

His bus driver, in fact, used to drill Miranda on the lyrics to popular songs. Some of his first favorites were Black Sheep's "A Wolf in Sheep's Clothing" and tracks by Queen Latifah and Naughty by Nature.

When Lin-Manuel was growing up in the 1980s and 1990s, hip-hop and rap were new forms of music that were becoming more popular. Lin-Manuel heard artists such as the Beastie Boys, Tupac Shakur, Biggie Smalls, and The Fat Boys in his early years. When Lin-Manuel was a boy, hip-hop was everywhere, and he absorbed it like a sponge. He loved its rhythms, the poetry of its lyrics, and, most of all, the stories it could tell. This new

9

Puerto Rico

Puerto Rico is an unincorporated territory of the United States 100 miles south of Florida. It consists of a small chain of islands. Puerto Rico is a territory of the United States, which means that, although some of Puerto Rico's finances come from the US government, the island is still independently governed. Citizens of Puerto Rico cannot vote in US elections, but they are allowed some of the benefits of being a part of the United States, such as health care. The nation has had a troubled existence, having been governed by Spain after its colonization in 1493 until 1898, when the United States won the territory in the Spanish American War. Because the island is located in the Caribbean, it is a popular tourist destination, despite the many earthquakes and hurricanes that the area has survived.

Today, the nation is still troubled. Many of its citizens have immigrated to the United States. But most still visit family in Puerto Rico, much like Miranda did as a child. Parts of the island are popular for wealthy vacationers. Other parts are impoverished and struggle for basic supplies and food. So many Puerto Ricans have moved to New York City that they have been dubbed "New Yoricans," meaning New Yorkers who are also Puerto Rican, much like the Mirandas. There is a massive Puerto Rican Day parade in Manhattan every year to celebrate its heritage. Many musicals, including Lin-Manuel's *In the Heights* (which includes characters from Cuba and the Dominican Republic as well) and Leonard Bernstein's *West Side Story*, were written about the musical and cultural influence that Puerto Ricans have had on New York culture.

style of music would go on to not only influence music and pop culture but also, eventually, even Broadway.

From a young age, it was clear that Lin-Manuel was destined for the stage. In the third

> **"I remember going to a Christmas concert once and throughout the concert he embodied the music and he had this aura around him."**

grade, he created a video for a presentation on a book report, in which he reenacted some of the book's major plot points and characters.[3] There are many videos of young Lin-Manuel dancing, singing, and even rapping. Miranda posts them on social media, in an effort to encourage others to follow their dreams. Videos include him performing in musicals and shows in high school and college as well as home videos. He has no problem poking fun at himself.

Miranda's parents raised him to be proud of his heritage. Today, Miranda often appears at events with his parents, and he also supports their charity and political works.

Those who knew Lin-Manuel when he was a child knew that music would play a big part in his life. His mother remembers one particular performance in which she knew her son was especially connected to music: "I remember going to a Christmas concert once and throughout the concert he embodied the music and he had this aura around him. And I remember leaving that church and wondering, 'Did anybody else just see the show I saw? Because it was amazing.' So he brings that magnetism to the stage every time, and I saw it when he was about ten years old."[4]

An Introduction to Theater

Lin-Manuel attended Hunter College Elementary School, a school for intellectually gifted students. Hunter College runs the elementary school, which is connected to a high school of the same name. The schools are located on the Upper East Side of Manhattan and are notoriously difficult to be accepted into. Some say it is more difficult for children to get into Hunter College Elementary and High School than it is to get into Ivy League universities. There are only fifty children enrolled in each grade. Both schools are consistently ranked among the top schools in the nation.

Along with rigorous academics, Lin-Manuel received music lessons as well. He was encouraged to play many instruments, in addition to the piano. Today, Miranda still plays piano when he writes his songs. He thanks his music teachers for his career and inspiration today: "The impact of arts education on my career is complete, total, and it saved my life. I had the good fortune to go to a magnet school in New York called Hunter and I went there from elementary through high school. There, my life was really changed by an elementary school music teacher named Barbara Ames."[5]

> "The impact of arts education on my career is complete, total, and it saved my life."

In elementary and middle school, Miranda was exposed to musical theater in a whole new way. The school was known for its sixth-grade productions. After having performed *West Side Story*, *Fiddler on the Roof*, *The Wizard of Oz*, *Peter Pan*, *Bye Bye Birdie*, and *Oklahoma*, there didn't seem many types of shows that the school wouldn't perform. By the time Lin-Manuel was in the sixth grade, the students wondered what performance they would put on. Having run out of age-appropriate plays, the teachers at Hunter decided to do a summer intensive where the students would write their

Political Influences

Since Lin-Manuel was a child, he'd been exposed to politics. His father worked for the Democratic Party in New York City as a consultant. During Lin-Manuel's childhood, his father worked for the mayor of New York City, Ed Koch. Luis A. Miranda Jr. had graduated from college in Puerto Rico before he turned eighteen, then immigrated to New York City to pursue a graduate degree at New York University. For the mayor, the elder Miranda worked as a special advisor to Hispanic affairs. He then cofounded a political consultant company, MirRam Group. Luz Miranda, Lin-Manuel's sister, now works for the company.

Because his family members are immigrants, the American political system was an important subject that was stressed in the household. They believed in the American Dream, and they were proud to vote in every election. During summer breaks throughout high school, Lin-Manuel worked at his father's office. He saw firsthand the American political system at work. It excited and fascinated him.

Even though his father had hopes for his talented and bright son to become a lawyer, Lin-Manuel knew that's not where his talents lay. Instead, he wrote jingles for his father's clients, including one for Eliot Spitzer's 2006 campaign for governor of New York. Because of his upbringing saturated with politics, Miranda has always been fascinated by the American system. Perhaps that is why, on a whim, he picked up Ron Chernow's biography *Alexander Hamilton* for some light beach reading.

Miranda is a known super fan of Aaron Sorkin's television drama *The West Wing* (1999–2006). So much, in fact, that on his final night of performing Alexander Hamilton in his massively successful hip-hop musical *Hamilton*, the orchestra played the theme song for the television show while he took his final bow.

So, it seems politics are in Miranda's blood. It should come as no surprise that he would revolutionize Broadway with a hip-hop musical about the beginnings of American politics.

own musical. However, the students, including Lin-Manuel, weren't as excited as the staff had hoped. They found rehearsals and the writing process difficult, to say the least. Finally, there was a compromise, in which the students would perform numbers from the previous six years' musicals, in addition to four numbers written by the sixth grade class. The piece was called *Four Plus Six, by the Sixth Grade*, and it was four hours long! It was a great experience for the soon-to-be star. "I got to write a short musical," he remembers. "I played Conrad Birdie, a cowhand in *Oklahoma*, a son in *Fiddler on the Roof*, Captain Hook in *Peter Pan*, Bernardo in *West Side Story*, and an Addaperle backup in the *Wizard of Oz/The Wiz*."[6]

Clearly, the experience changed the young Lin-Manuel Miranda. "This is a very lethal dosage of musical theater at a very young age. I got to literally play all of the parts and I realized that it was the best time of my life."[7]

This experience created a fire in Lin-Manuel Miranda. As he entered high school, he focused more and more on theater and music. He no longer thought of the school year in the two-semester split. Instead, he focused on the play in the fall, the musical in the winter, and then the student-run theater group in the spring and summer. "That was the focus of my creative efforts for as long as I can remember," he has said.[8] This clearly influenced Miranda's high school career. He was known around the school for his love of music and for carrying his boom box with him everywhere, so he could play music and perform whenever the occasion called for it (and sometimes when it didn't!). This was also when he began to freestyle rap, a skill he would develop and utilize for the rest of his career.

He played the Pirate King in *Pirates of Penzance* and Judas in *Godspell*. He assistant-directed a performance of *A Chorus Line* and directed a production of *West Side Story*. He also began writing songs and short musicals. It was clear that young Lin-Manuel was hooked on theater, and there was little hope of him focusing on anything else.

CHAPTER TWO

Wesleyan Years

• •

I n 1998, Lin-Manuel Miranda graduated from Hunter College High School and began attending Wesleyan University. Wesleyan is a liberal arts college in Connecticut that focuses on giving its students a superior education in the liberal arts and sciences.

His parents didn't want their son to focus all his studies on music and theater; they hoped he would be exposed to other interests in college. Instead, however, Miranda decided to major in theater studies and film. Gradually, film became less and less of a focus, as it became more clear that theater, particularly musical theater, was his passion.

Studying the Classics

As a theater studies major, Lin-Manuel studied every aspect of theater, from performance to music, directing, history, and even set design. Miranda performed in many of Wesleyan's musicals and plays, such as *Jesus Christ: Superstar*, and created a student-run production of *Seven Minutes in Heaven*, a play

Being a Theater Major

Studying theater in a conservatory or college setting is not like being in your school's annual musical. Students of theater study acting in many different styles and techniques. They also study dance, like ballet and jazz, as well as music. Many theater students also play musical instruments such as piano, guitar, and violin.

But aside from learning how to perform, many theater majors must learn the "behind the scenes" work of theater. They not only perform in their school's productions but are required to work as stage managers, ushers, and even on lighting and set design. They study theater history from the days of the ancient Greeks to modern plays such as Miranda's *Hamilton*. Most theater majors graduate with an immense knowledge of all aspects of theater, from history to backstage to performance. Many theater majors go on to work in theater, film, and television. Not all of them become performers, however. Some become casting agents or managers, directors, set designers, costume designers, makeup artists, film editors, and music directors.

There are special schools, called conservatories, where students only study performance. Unlike theater majors in colleges and universities, these students do not study literature, mathematics, science, or social studies. They only study music, acting, or dance. Some well-known English-speaking theater conservatories include the American Academy of Dramatic Arts in New York and Los Angeles, the Royal Academy of Dramatic Arts in London, the American Musical and Dramatic Academy in New York and Los Angeles, and the Julliard School in New York City. But there are conservatories all over the world, in almost every language, proving that entertainment defies language and can be appreciated across the world.

he had drafted in high school. He also directed a few productions, work that would prove helpful when creating his original musicals in the years following.[1]

At Wesleyan, he studied the greats of Broadway such as Stephen Sondheim, Andrew Lloyd-Webber, Leonard Bernstein, George Gershwin, and Rodgers and Hammerstein. He also studied straight plays, such as those by Sophocles, William Shakespeare, Tony Kushner, David Mamet, Eugene O'Neill, Neil Simon, Tom Stoppard, and Sam Shepard. This gave Miranda a well-rounded theater experience and prepared him for the world of theater that he was about to enter. He already had an immense knowledge of musical theater and pop culture, but learning about the classics helped Miranda to appreciate theater all the more.

More Than Theater

But Miranda wasn't just interested in theater. Music had always been a passion of his. Even from a young age, Miranda had a knack for learning and creating lyrics.

During his first weeks at college, Miranda met Anthony Veneziale, who would go on to be a lifelong collaborator.[2] The two young men bonded over their shared love of diverse music, their passion for making music, and their aspirations for life on Broadway. Soon after, they met others with their aspirations and talents, and began an improvisation, or improv, rap group called Freestyle Love Supreme.

Their premise was based on their love of improv theater, which asks actors to create a show without a script. Essentially, the performers are improvising their lines based off of audience suggestions or a rough sketch of ideas. Improv theater is hardly new. *Saturday Night Live* and *Mad TV* have taken improv and sketch comedy into the average household. But what Freestyle Love Supreme did was different: it created hip-hop musical numbers based off the idea of improv theater.

Freestyle rap is a similar idea, in that none of the lyrics are written beforehand. An artist must create a musical number based off an idea, a suggestion, or a bit of momentary inspiration. And Freestyle Love Supreme took Miranda's love of skilled hip-hop and improv theater, with a recurring group of performers, and combined it all.

Freestyle Love Supreme's performances were immediately a hit. And the group has been together

Freestyle Love Supreme is a hip-hop improv group that Miranda began in college. The group includes Anthony Veneziale (*left*), Christopher Jackson (*center*), and Miranda (*right*), and still performs in public when they can.

• • • • • • • • • • • • • • • • • • • •

ever since. Members have come and gone, but Freestyle Love Supreme still performs in New York City regularly. The group's shows are funny, poignant, timely, and always entertaining. "It's crazy to think about how long we've been performing as a group," Miranda said in a press release about a performance in 2016. "The number of boy bands we've outlived in that time is staggering! No matter what happens in each of our lives, we all come back to 'Freestyle Love Supreme.' It's our touchstone..."[3] Miranda continues to use his friends from Freestyle Love Supreme to create his music. Christopher Jackson, a graduate of the American Music and Drama Academy, has been involved in both of Miranda's original musicals and joined Freestyle Love Supreme not long after meeting Miranda during casting for *In the Heights*. He, as well as Miranda and Veneziale, still perform with the group. Daveed Diggs is also now a member of the group. Tom Kail works as the group's director.

Miranda was able to combine his abilities for creating lyrics and his quick wit in a way that was entertaining and entirely new. It is a gift he has continued to use throughout his life.

Miranda is also known for his love of pop culture. He loves television shows (he's known for being a big fan of the television show *The West Wing*) and reads many different types of books, from histories and biographies to fantasy and science fiction. He also loves to play video games, such as *Grand Theft Auto*. His diverse taste in music is also well-known. He absorbs what is happening around him, and he uses it to help create his art. It was a talent he began to develop in college and continues to use to this day.

Writing and Collaborating

Perhaps the most amazing thing that Miranda did while he was in college was that he began to write his own musical. He had written short productions as a child and teenager. And he was a founding member of his own freestyle rap improv group. But at just twenty years old, Miranda had more of his own ideas than could be put in one or two numbers. He had enough ideas to create a full-length musical.

As with many musicals, *In the Heights* began as a few plot lines and a song or two in its author's mind. He was inspired by the streets in which he'd grown up, and the culture with which he'd been surrounded in his youth. He'd read the works of Puerto Rican writer Quiara Alegria Hudes, and he worked closely with her in order to develop the plot of his play.[4] He wanted to bring Washington Heights to Broadway, to show the world his exceptionally artistic background, and how special a place really could be. "In the winter of 1999, I applied to put up a new show in the student-run '92 Theater. At the time, I had one song and a title: *In the Heights*. I was given the theater for the weekend of April 20–22," says Miranda of the beginnings of *In the Heights*. "I just wrote. I put in all the things I'd always wanted to see onstage: propulsive freestyle rap scenes outside of bodegas, salsa numbers that also revealed character and story. I tried to write the kind of show I'd want to be in."[5] The show broke box-office records for the '92 Theater that year.

> **"I just wrote. I put in all the things I'd always wanted to see onstage: propulsive freestyle rap scenes outside of bodegas, salsa numbers that also revealed character and story. I tried to write the kind of show I'd want to be in."**

After the performance, Thomas Kail, John Buffalo Mailer (son of Norman Mailer), and Neil Stewart, all Wesleyan students, approached Miranda to see if he was

Thomas Kail (*left*) and Lin-Manuel Miranda met as students at Wesleyan College. The two would go on to collaborate on two successful musicals: *In the Heights* and *Hamilton*.

interested in taking the show to Broadway. They were planning on creating a production company after they graduated that spring. And they wanted Miranda and *In the Heights* for one of their first productions. Of course, he was excited by the prospect. The group worked on the musical even more, hoping to get the attention of producers.

Workshopping is the process by which a musical gets refined. A piece is taken in its entirety and is casually performed in front of an audience of trusted and knowledgeable peers. Sometimes the process starts with a group of actors sitting around a table to

Wesleyan University

Wesleyan University is a liberal arts college in Middleton, Connecticut. It emphasizes an education in the arts and sciences, but also offers post-graduate studies in many disciplines. It offers PhD (or doctorate) programs in biology, chemistry, mathematics and computer science, molecular biology and biochemistry, music, and physics. It was founded as an all-male college in 1831 with the intention of it becoming an Episcopal Seminary. It became one of the first American universities to create a comprehensive undergraduate science program. It remained a small university (with only a few hundred students) until the 1970s, when it became larger than its peer universities Williams College and Amherst College.

In the 1950s, as Wesleyan was expanding, the university's then-president Victor Lloyd Butterfield began restructuring the college's education system. Under his guidance, the students were divided into smaller schools that specialized in certain areas of study, such as literature, science, and the arts. Currently, the university offers forty-six fields of undergraduate academic study and thirteen interdisciplinary degrees. Among those interdisciplinary studies are the College of Social Studies, which combines history, economics, philosophy, and government; the College of Letters, which combines history, literature, philosophy, and foreign language; the College of the Environment, which combines science and environmental studies;

and the College of Integrative Sciences, which combines science and technology. Other main areas of study at the university include Applied Mathematics and Science (including Astronomy), Film, Theater, Music, and International Study. Wesleyan consistently ranks among the top ten universities in the United States in terms of academics.

The university occupies a 360-acre (1.5 km^2) campus in Middleton, with over 340 buildings, which include residential dormitories, laboratories, lecture halls, an observatory, and an eleven-building Center for the Arts. There are no cars allowed on campus, and students and faculty must leave the campus by public bus.

Among Wesleyan's well-known alumni are filmmakers Michael Bay, Joss Whedon, and Paul Weitz; author Daniel Handler (also known as Lemony Snicket); Ben Goldwasser and Andrew VanWyngarden of MGMT; Super Bowl–winning New England Patriots coach Bill Belichick; and actress Dana Delany. Among its renowned faculty are Woodrow Wilson, T. S. Eliot, and Nobel Prize for Medicine–winner Satoshi Omura.

read a script. When a musical is being written, those actors are often also musicians who perform songs from the show. Feedback is given on what works and what doesn't, in order to make the play have the strongest impact on an audience. After appropriate revisions to the script, the play is often brought "to its feet," meaning that the actors begin to perform their parts on a stage. There is more feedback from peers after that. The workshopping process can take years. It is common practice among new plays, to ensure that the play will be as good as it can be.

After workshopping his musical, Miranda realized it needed more local flavor. So, he added more hip-hop, more salsa numbers, and more neighborhood locations such as bodegas and urban neighborhood convenience stores. After several drafts, it was ready to be performed. Five drafts and two years later, the musical was ready for the eyes of Broadway.

But as Miranda was working on *In the Heights*, he still had to finish his education. He graduated in 2002 from Wesleyan University, with an original musical under his belt, and was ready to face the world of Broadway head-on.

CHAPTER THREE

In the Heights

• •

I n 2005, after four years of drafting and revising, *In the Heights* was performed off-Broadway, in Connecticut's Eugene O'Neill Theater for the National Theater Conference. Not only did the performance spark rave reviews but it caught the attention of many producers who wanted to bring the show to Broadway.

It was unlike anything that had been done on Broadway before. Much like Jonathan Larson's *Rent* in the 1990s, *In the Heights* combined the natural vibrancy of New York City's neighborhoods with music that was not only inspired by popular music and culture of the time but that was also catchy. Miranda had seen *Rent* when he was in high school, and it had a heavy influence on his writing. It can be heard in many of Miranda's songs from both *In the Heights* and *Hamilton*. Miranda describes *Rent* as "a revelation—that you could write about now, and you could have musicals that really felt contemporary."[1]

It is easy to see how this would influence Miranda and his work. For indeed, he has continued the work of Jonathan Larson to bring the idea of the Broadway musical into a more realistic and contemporary state. But aside from the two musicals being representations of New York City neighborhoods during their time, the two musicals also refuse to shy away from social and political issues. *Rent* is well-known for celebrating the LGBTQ community and bringing awareness to the AIDS epidemic of the 1980s and 1990s. *In the Heights* discusses immigrants' issues, as well as the financial difficulties facing many average American families who are desperately trying to achieve the American Dream.

The Story of a Neighborhood

In the Heights is very much the story of a neighborhood. Much like the Upper West Side of *West Side Story* and the East Village of *Rent*, *In the Heights* follows a cast of characters in a particular New York City neighborhood through their trials, tribulations, and triumphs. Characters in the show include a bodega owner, a college student returning from Stanford University, a taxi driver, a hairdresser, and many immigrants to the neighborhood of Washington Heights.

Unlike *West Side Story* or *Rent*, however, *In the Heights* focuses on a microcosm of a neighborhood—an area spanning just three blocks. The show takes place over just three days—over Fourth of July weekend. There are struggles with money, family, and love. There are moments in which characters dream of a better life (such as in the number "96,000" in which one character wins the lottery and every person in the whole neighborhood dreams of what they would do with that

On June 15, 2008, Lin-Manuel Miranda and the rest of the cast of *In the Heights* performed at the 62nd Annual Tony Awards in New York City. Miranda would win his first Tony that night.

• •

amount of money), and moments in which they celebrate the life they have (such as "Paciencia y Fe," in which the Cuban matriarch of the neighborhood sings about her emigration from Cuba). There are even moments of chaos when the power goes out throughout the city.

Miranda originated the role of Usnavi, the play's narrator and one of its central characters. Usnavi owns a bodega on the corner and has spent his whole life in the neighborhood. He is named Usnavi because as his parents entered New York Harbor on a boat from Cuba, the first boat they saw read "U.S. Navy." Other characters include Vanessa, Usnavi's love interest and a hairdresser who dreams of a studio apartment in the West Village; Abuela Claudia, who is the matriarch of the neighborhood; and Nina Rosario, a student returning home after a failed year at Stanford University. Christopher Jackson helped create the role of Benny, a taxi dispatcher who doesn't speak any English.

New York City is its own character in the show: the ebb and flow of people moving in and out of an area, the rhythm of its streets, and the full-of-life diversity

Miranda and Kail wanted the show to be as authentic as possible. One of the set's important locations is Usnavi's bodega.

that every New Yorker faces every day. From graffiti artists to immigrants to death and the celebration of life, *In the Heights* showcases what is best (and worst) about growing up in a close-knit urban neighborhood. It is a show that is uniquely New York and uniquely of Miranda's generation. It was directly inspired by his own upbringing. Says Miranda about his first full-length musical: "It was everything I'd always wanted to see in a musical. It was Latino characters."[2]

But Miranda admits that although *In the Heights* may have been his idea, it didn't come to fruition until he'd met his collaborators. When he met Thomas Kail, the play was brought to a new level. Miranda says that collaborating is

The Most Successful Broadway Musicals of All Time

There are many ways to determine a successful Broadway musical: highest gross sales, longest run on Broadway (which is affectionately dubbed "the Great White Way"), and, of course, a large fan base. Here is a list of fifteen of the most successful Broadway shows in recent history.

The Lion King, opened November 13, 1997 (the third-longest running show on Broadway), gross ticket sales (as of 2017) $1.32 billion

The Phantom of the Opera, opened January 26, 1988 (the longest-running show on Broadway), gross ticket sales (as of 2017) $1.08 billion

Wicked, opened October 30, 2003, gross ticket sales (as of 2017) $1.06 billion

Mamma Mia, October 18, 2001–September 12, 2015, gross ticket sales $624.6 million

Chicago (revival) opened November 4, 1996 (the second-longest running show on Broadway), gross ticket sales (as of 2017) $568.4 million

Jersey Boys, November 6, 2005–January 15, 2017, gross ticket sales $548.8 million

The Book of Mormon, opened March 24, 2011, gross ticket sales (as of 2017), $455.7 million

Beauty and the Beast, April 8, 1994–July 29, 2007, gross ticket sales $429.2 million

Les Misérables (original), March 12, 1987–May 8, 2003, gross sales $406.3 million

Cats, October 7, 1982—September 10, 2000 (the fourth-longest run in Broadway history), gross ticket sales (as of 2017) $366.4 million

Mary Poppins, November 16, 2006–March 3, 2013, gross ticket sales $296.4 million

The Producers, April 29, 2001–April 22, 2007, gross ticket sales $288.4 million

Miss Saigon, April 11, 1991–January 28, 2001, gross ticket sales $285.8 million

Rent, April 29, 1996–September 7, 2008, gross ticket sales $274.2 million

Hairspray, August 15, 2002–January 4, 2009, gross ticket sales $252.2 million[3]

This, of course, doesn't include classics like *A Chorus Line*, *Fiddler on the Roof*, *Jesus Christ Superstar*, *My Fair Lady*, *the Sound of Music*, *Annie*, and other classics that have made their mark on pop culture and American music, but is merely based on top ticket sales and number of performances. *Hamilton* has broken many records, including most Tony Award nominations, and has shot to massive popularity in a very short time, but it has yet to break records for top-grossing sales or longest run. It has a long way to go before it breaks those records.

what has helped him come so far. "Tommy Kail, who by all accounts is smarter than me and had fifty ideas of how to make the musical better. Then we found the people who could help us really bring it to life, and that was Alex Lacamoire, our music director, and crucially, Quiara Hudes, our book writer, who had the same upbringing and schism growing up in northern Philly that I did in northern Manhattan. We really doubled down on, 'Okay, let's make this about our community, and a love letter to the communities we grew up in.'"[4]

> "Let's make this about our community, and a love letter to the communities we grew up in."

A Smash Hit

In the Heights began previews at the Richard Rodgers Theatre on 46th Street in New York City on February 14, 2008. It opened officially two weeks later. Kail continued in his role of director, and most of the original off-Broadway cast continued performing the roles they helped to bring to life. The show was billed as an "original hip-hop-salsa-merengue musical about two days in the life of Washington Heights, a vibrant immigrant neighborhood at the top of Manhattan."[5]

After just a few months on Broadway, theater's biggest show, the Tony Awards, announced its nominations. *In the Heights* was nominated an amazing thirteen times.

The 62nd Tony Awards ceremony was held in Radio City Music Hall on June 15, 2008. Whoopi Goldberg hosted the event. *In the Heights* won four out of its thirteen

Theater's Biggest Night: The Tony Awards

Music has the Grammy Awards. Film has the Oscars. And theater has the Tony Awards. The Antoinette Perry Award for Excellence in Theater, more commonly known as the Tony, recognizes and celebrates the year in theater. The awards show is filled with performances from its nominees and celebrates the writers, costume designers, musicians, directors, actors, and everyone that works to make a show a success. The show takes place annually in June in New York City. The Tonys are considered the highest honor in American theater. They are presented by the Broadway League and the American Theater Wing, and began in 1947 with eleven categories. But as shows have evolved to reflect pop culture, the Tonys have grown to have twenty-four categories.

Winners are chosen by a committee of judges appointed by the American Theater Wing, the Broadway League, and Dramatists Guild, Actors' Equity Association, United Scenic Artists, and the Society of Stage Directors and Choreographers. The rotating group of professionals are well-known in the world of theater and are considered experts in their respective fields, whether that is music, choreography, acting, design, directing, or writing.

The Tonys only celebrate Broadway shows. A Broadway show is defined as being in a theater that holds more than five hundred seats, not necessarily that it is performed in New York City, although the Tonys have notoriously reflected New York theater. Performing at the Tonys is a considerable honor. Lin-Manuel Miranda has done it twice for shows of his own creation.

When Miranda won his first Tony, he proudly waved a Puerto Rican flag to honor his heritage.

nominations: Best Musical, Best Original Score, Best Orchestrations, and Best Choreography. Lin-Manuel Miranda suddenly found himself among theater's most elite class of writers and performers. *In the Heights* also won a Grammy that year for Best Musical Show Album, and it was nominated for a Pulitzer Prize. The cast of *In the Heights* performed a mash up of numbers from their hit show, "In the Heights / 96,000."

Shortly after the Tony Awards, *In the Heights* went on an international North American tour. And then it was brought to theaters in Peru, the Philippines, Panama, Japan, and the West End in London, England.

Despite its praise and awards, however, Miranda is proudest of the fact that he brought awareness to his culture and brought it into a mainly white art form. Latinos finally got to see themselves on Broadway in a role that didn't involve them fighting, dealing drugs, or holding a knife. One aspect of the play is that it shows a side of the Latino culture that isn't often depicted in mainstream theater, film, or television. It depicts the story of immigrants who work hard in order to give their families a better opportunity than they ever had, and also the children of those parents, who want to honor it.⁶

And a Grammy, Too!

The Tonys may be theater's biggest night, but there's no doubt that the Grammys are music's biggest night. The annual ceremony recognized outstanding achievements in music in the mainly English-language industry. The show takes place at the Staples Center in Los Angeles and also features performances by the nominees.

On February 8, 2009, the original cast recording of *In the Heights* won the Grammy award for Best Musical Show. It was a dream come true for Miranda, the kid from Washington Heights that had always loved music.

Outside of Theater

Although theater is perhaps Miranda's passion, he has a life outside of the theater. He worked as a high school English teacher while workshopping *In the Heights*. He also wrote jingles for his father's political contacts and performed at weddings and bar mitzvahs. He is also a notorious family man, spending time with his parents, sister, and grandparents. Loyal to a fault, Miranda continued to work with his friends who had helped him create a musical, and he was looking to the future, not sure exactly what his next big project was.

CHAPTER FOUR

"My Shot": Making More Music

• • • • • • • • • • • • • • • • •

I n 2010, Miranda married Vanessa Adriana Nadal, with whom he'd attended high school. When he was a senior, she was a sophomore, and he had a crush on the beautiful Latina. "She was gorgeous and I'm famously bad at talking to women I find attractive," said Miranda of his future wife.[1] Nadal was not necessarily an artist like her future husband, however. She studied a lot. Mathematics was her favorite subject. But she was a great dancer, and she loved music. She also was from Washington Heights. After graduating high school, Miranda went off to Connecticut to attend Wesleyan, and thought little of the beautiful girl from Hunter College High School as he focused on his education and creating *In the Heights*. For her part, Nadal went on to study at Massachusetts Institute of Technology (MIT), and began working as a scientist at Johnson & Johnson in New Jersey.

Lin-Manuel Miranda and his wife, Vanessa Nadal, often appear at red-carpet events together. They both have busy careers, but they support each other through everything. The two had a son, Sebastian, in November of 2014.

• •

The two reconnected on Facebook in 2005, when he invited her to see him perform in Freestyle Love Supreme. Within a few weeks, the two were dating. Miranda was impressed by Nadal's mind, and she was impressed by his creativity. While he was finishing *In the Heights*, Nadal was attending Fordham Law School. She graduated in the spring of 2010.

At their wedding in September of that year, a chorus of Broadway singers sang during the ceremony. And the reception was everything you'd expect a Broadway wedding to be. Many of the guests performed: singing, rapping, and improvising. Perhaps the most noteworthy performance of the evening, however, was when Miranda and his groomsmen created a flash-mob performance of "To Life" from *Fiddler on the Roof.*[2]

The Music Man

Although he'd won Tonys and a Grammy, Miranda was still relatively unknown. He was never stopped on the street or surrounded by paparazzi. He was still able to maintain some anonymity.

> **"I'm famously bad at talking to women I find attractive."**

Occasionally, someone who happened to have seen the show or who was a big fan of Broadway theater would approach him. But it wasn't a daily occurrence.

Miranda took a little time off from performing on stage after the success of *In the Heights*. He cowrote the music and lyrics for *Bring It On: The Musical*, based on the popular teen film about a cheerleading squad. It had a limited run at the St. James Theater in New York City and was nominated for two Tonys, including Best Musical and Best Choreography. It didn't win, however, and is not considered a great success.

Andy Blankenbuehler (*left*), Lin-Manuel Miranda, and Thomas Kitt (*right*) take a bow during the opening night of *Bring It On: The Musical.*

Soon after, Miranda began making guest appearances on television shows. He appeared in the episode "Good Cop, Bad Dog" of *Modern Family*. In 2012, he played "Reggie" in *The Odd Life of Timothy Green*. He also appeared in the episode "Bedtime

Vanessa Nadal

Lin-Manuel Miranda says his wife is the only reason anything gets done. "She nudges me towards promise by degrees. She is a perfect symphony of one. Our son is her most beautiful reprise."[3] Nadal studied chemical engineering at the Massachusetts Institute of Technology and worked as a research and development scientist for Johnson & Johnson. She also earned a law degree from Fordham University. The two seem to be perfect opposites.

Although the two met in high school, they didn't begin a romantic relationship until much later. Nadal, whose mother is an Austrian immigrant, focused on her education and her career, much like Miranda. It was only after the couple reconnected on Facebook after several years apart that their romance began.

Nadal loves *Grand Theft Auto*, which is Miranda's favorite video game. The two enjoy playing against each other at home. She is also well-known for making large breakfasts. Although she isn't a musician, she helps her husband through his creative process. Much has been said about the fact that *Hamilton* has several strong female characters, based on people who really lived. History often forgets about the women, and Miranda didn't want his hip-hop musical about the founding fathers to give females the same treatment. "Lin is attuned to the female roles, but I did push him a little bit," she said. "He's very empathetic and good at putting himself in other people's shoes and I think that's why he can write women in a way that other men can't."[4] The song "Helpless" from *Hamilton* was written for her, although when Miranda first played it for her, she told him to continue working on it.

Nadal gave birth to son, Sebastian, in 2014, just before *Hamilton* opened on Broadway. During his acceptance speech for his Tony Award, Miranda famously read a sonnet he had written for his wife. Though she prefers to stay mostly out of the spotlight, the two are darlings on red carpet events. "She knows she's dope," Miranda says about his wife. "She's beautiful but not vain. She's smart but not arrogant. It's like, all killer, no filler."[5] Nadal currently works as a litigation attorney at Jones Day, an international law firm in New York City.

Stories" of *How I Met Your Mother*, in which he plays a man riding the bus with one the of main characters, Marshall (played by Jason Segal), and he improvs a rap to entertain Marshall's baby. The following year, he had a recurring role on the NBC drama *Do No Harm*.

The exposure from film and television was good, but Miranda couldn't forget his love of the stage. He appeared in staged concerts and wrote short musical comedies, most notably *21 Chump Street* for the 2014 *This American Life* live show.

In 2009, Miranda received an honorary degree from Yeshiva University. He is the youngest person to ever

Alexander Hamilton, one of America's Founding Fathers, served as an unlikely source of inspiration for Miranda.

have that honor. Yeshiva University is a well-known college in Washington Heights.

Getting Inspired

Inspiration can strike from anywhere, or anything. It can come from something you see, read, hear, or even smell. For Miranda, inspiration came from reading a biography of Alexander Hamilton while on vacation. It is the kind of story that Broadway legends are made of. Ron Chernow's 2004 biography of the first secretary of the Treasury of the United States is a *New York Times* best seller and is a lengthy and detailed account of the founding father's life. And about fifty pages into reading it, an idea struck Miranda that there needed to be a musical written about the founding of America, specifically about this man who had accomplished so much in his short life.[6]

Before long, Miranda had written what would someday become the opening number of his mega hit hip-hop musical *Hamilton*. And he even had the nerve to perform the piece, only entitled "The Hamilton Mixtape" at the White House Poetry Jam in May 2009.[7]

Introducing the piece that he was performing before President Obama, he described Alexander Hamilton as the founding father who most embodied hip-hop, which of course, made the audience laugh.[8] The video, released on many press sources and YouTube, went viral within hours.

Some thought the idea was too far outside the mainstream to succeed. Many thought the concept would offend, or even disrespect, the legend and memory of the founding fathers. Others simply couldn't imagine how a hip-hop musical about the founding fathers would even work. But nonetheless, no one could deny that the strange idea was tremendously entertaining and intriguing. Miranda had found the inspiration for his next big project. And even he didn't know what would it would become, or how much he was about to change the world of the Broadway musical.

CHAPTER FIVE

Hamilton

· · · · · · · · · · · · · ·

I t took Lin-Manuel Miranda almost five years to write the musical that would shoot him into superstardom. He reached out to Ron Chernow, the author of *Hamilton*, the biography that had captivated him on his beach vacation, and to his surprise, Chernow was interested in Miranda's project. He helped Miranda get the historical details of the era correct in this hip-hop musical about the American Revolution.

The Dream Team

But Miranda didn't just enlist a biographer. He also worked with many of his contacts throughout the Broadway world. He brought Christopher Jackson on board again, as well as director Thomas Kail and musician Alex Lacamoire. Hoping to re-create the magic of *In the Heights*, Miranda surrounded himself with the people who had helped him before. This dream team of collaborators drafted and redrafted the songs for *Hamilton*. While the project was still in workshop form, Miranda called it the "Hamilton Mixtape." Originally, it

The Face on the $10 Bill

As the first secretary of the Treasury, and the man that created America's banking system, Alexander Hamilton has been on the U.S. $10 bill since the 1930s. Although he was not one of the better-known founding fathers, this was his legacy. The $10 bill has changed appearance many times since then, but Alexander Hamilton has remained the portrait on its face. In 2015, however, the United States Department of Treasury decided to change the $10 bill and replace Hamilton's portrait with a woman.

Jacob J. Lew, the current secretary of the Treasury, decided to keep Alexander Hamilton as the face of the $10 bill, due almost exclusively to the popularity of *Hamilton*. "Mr. Lew may have reneged on a commitment he made last year to make a woman the face of the $10 bill, opting instead to keep Alexander Hamilton, to the delight of a fan base swollen with enthusiasm over a Broadway rap musical based on the life of the first Treasury secretary".[17] Instead, it was decided that Andrew Jackson would be removed from the $20 bill, to be replaced by Harriet Tubman.

began as a concept album, as Miranda wasn't sure about the marketability of a hip-hop musical about Alexander Hamilton on stage.

But he knew this story had to be told in the unique way that only he could see and hear. He wanted to bring Alexander Hamilton to life again: to tell his own story, to remind America what it was that the founding fathers fought for. "[Alexander Hamilton] writes his way out of poverty. He writes his way into the war through just a war of ideas. He writes his way into [George] Washington's good graces. He also writes his way into trouble—at every step of the way, when cooler heads are not around him to prevail. I immediately made the leap to a hip-hop artist writing about his circumstances and transcending them."[1]

He worked relentlessly on the mixtape, drafting songs and rewriting them to better reflect the people that would have sung them. He read historical documents and letters from the founding fathers themselves, just so he could get their words, phrasing, and personalities as truly reflective of the individuals as possible. Alexander Hamilton, the show's protagonist and the character that Miranda portrayed, raps in dense, stream-of-consciousness phrasing. The songs of Thomas Jefferson and King George are more along the lines of what one would expect from a Broadway show: sweeping melodies with belting voices and catchy phrases. George Washington's numbers are authoritarian, yet humble. The songs of the Marquise de Lafayette begin with the character struggling with the English language, and by the end of the first act, he has the fastest raps of any of the other performers, which reflects Lafayette's rise to becoming a general in the American Revolution. Aaron Burr's songs are thoughtful and emotional.

If one listens closely to the music of *Hamilton* and knows what he or she is listening for, he or she can hear the influences of Miranda's musical life. "The Story of Tonight" is clearly an homage to "La Vie Boheme" from

Rent. "History Has Its Eyes on You" shows influences of *Les Miserables.* Miranda tips his hat to all of his musical influences from R&B, classic rock, and pop, seamlessly telling the story of the birth of a nation. "You'll Be Back," sung by King George, has all the hallmarks of a 1960's pop song written by John Lennon and Paul McCartney. The cabinet battles are perhaps some of Lin-Manuel Miranda's most epic songs. During these numbers, the founding fathers actually have a "rap battle" to demonstrate debating issues of slavery, the economy, and how a nation should be run. While it is hard to imagine the very white founding fathers rapping about their differences, hearing the issues performed in this way brings the debates to life in the twenty-first century and helps the audience connect with the reality of what it was like for this group of rebels to decide how to run a nation.

Perhaps the most amazing thing about *Hamilton* is that a story about the very white founding fathers works with a hip-hop beat. "I'm not sure if Lin's a genius. Hamilton was a genius," Chernow says. "But Lin's made a masterpiece."[2] Audience members agree: the show makes people question what they are seeing, what they think about their perceptions of the founding fathers. It makes them laugh, cry, and have empathy for people they've never even considered before.

The Cast

Of course, part of *Hamilton*'s success is due to its stellar original cast. Lin-Manuel Miranda, naturally, originated the role of Alexander Hamilton. But he wasn't the only

Broadway star involved with the show. Leslie Odom Jr. (who starred in *Rent*) played Aaron Burr. Phillipa Soo starred as Hamilton's wife, Eliza. Renée Elise Goldsberry played Angelica Schuyler-Church, her older sister. Daveed Diggs played both the Marquise de Lafayette and Thomas Jefferson. Christopher Jackson played the role of George Washington; Okieriete Onaodowan played Hercules Mulligan and James Madison. The role of King George III went to Jonathan Groff (of *Spring Awakening* and *Glee* fame). All were well-known in the music and theater worlds but had yet to become household names. *Hamilton* changed that for them all.

Miranda took a bow with castmates after the premiere performance of *Hamilton* at The Public Theater in February 2015. He was surprised that his latest project was such a hit and was moved by the fact that it touched so many audience members.

Perhaps the most incredible thing about the cast of *Hamilton* is that even though it is the story of a group of all-white English colonists, the story is told through a multicultural eye. Nearly every major role is portrayed by a person who wouldn't normally be cast in the role of a traditionally white story. The cast members include Hispanics, Asian Americans, African Americans, and people of mixed race. Broadway has for many years been a predominately white art form. Musicals such as *Porgy and Bess*, *Show Boat*, *The King and I*, and *West Side Story* began to bring people of color to the Broadway stage. But well over half a century later, Broadway rarely represented the diversity of America. But *Hamilton*, and Lin-Manuel Miranda's casting of it, was meant to represent America's population in a time when many minorities felt underrepresented. Perhaps that was the point: to show the story of the United States of America in a way that is approachable to the average American.

Alexander Hamilton

For centuries, Alexander Hamilton was one of the more mysterious founding fathers. Shot in a duel before he was fifty years old, he didn't live to see the nation he'd fought so hard to build. Born on the island of Nevis (now St. Croix) in the Caribbean as the illegitimate child of a Scotsman and a woman who was separated from her husband, no one had many expectations for the young Hamilton. His father abandoned him at an early age, and before he was ten years old, his mother had died of a severe fever. By the time he was eleven years old, he was working for an import-export shipping business between the colonies and Europe. By the time he was fourteen, he was running it.

He immigrated to New York (still then one of the British colonies) in 1772, just before the American Revolution. It was there that he began his formal education at King's College (now Columbia University) and met many of the people who would change the fate of the United States of America, including the Marquise de Lafayette, Thomas Jefferson, James Madison, and, of course, his lifelong frenemy Aaron Burr. By the time he was twenty years old, the Revolution was in full swing, and the young Alexander Hamilton was working as the secretary for George Washington, fighting against the British to make America a free, independent nation.

After helping to win the Revolutionary War, Alexander Hamilton became a lawyer and went on to help write *The Federalist Papers* and the U.S. Constitution, created the U.S. Mint, and served as the first secretary of the Treasury. He created the banking system of the United States and all but eliminated the young nation's postwar debt.[3] He was lauded as a brilliant mind of his time, but was also known for being divisive. He did not shy away from speaking his opinions, nor from defending his own honor. He created the first political sex scandal in American history. He opposed slavery and dreamed of America becoming an industrialized nation. He wrote all the time. Many of his original writings survive today, including letters, journal entries, and of course the "Reynolds Pamphlet," along with notes he used to draft his many political documents. A New Yorker, an immigrant, and one of the most famous men in America during his lifetime, Alexander Hamilton was a testament to what the United States was supposed to be: a place where anyone from anywhere from any walk of life could come and make a name for himself or herself.

In 1804, before the United States of America had even had a chance to fully realize its potential and prove itself on the world stage, Alexander Hamilton was shot and killed in a duel in Weehawken, New Jersey, by a man he'd known half his life, Aaron Burr. Mortally wounded over an insult, he refused to fire back. He had been somewhat lost to history before Ron Chernow wrote his now-famous biography on the least-known founding father. And then Lin-Manuel Miranda read it and created the most popular musical in modern Broadway history. Forgotten no more, Alexander Hamilton is now America's favorite founding father and will never be forgotten to history again. In fact, over two hundred years after his death, Alexander Hamilton is still making history.

The Public Theater

It took Miranda five years to write *Hamilton*, and after creating the mixtape, he wanted to see if he could make it into a play. He began promoting his project by performing it. In 2012, he performed sections of the "Hamilton Mixtape" at the Allen Room in New York City.[4] At the time, few people knew what to make of it. A *New York Times* review asked its readers,

> Is "The Hamilton Mixtape," from which 12 numbers were performed, a future Broadway

musical? A concept album? A multimedia extravaganza in search of a platform? Does it even matter? What it is, is hot. Its language is a seamless marriage of hip-hop argot and raw American history made startlingly alive; the music arranged for a sextet by Alex Lacamoire is flexible, undigitized hip-hop rock fusion.[5]

In January 2015, the show made its way to the Public Theater in New York City. It was slotted for a short run at first, just two months. But it quickly became a phenomenon. "Lin-Manuel Miranda is a marvel, but nothing could have prepared us for the astonishing achievement of *Hamilton*," Oskar Eustis, the artistic director of the Public Theater, said about the show when it premiered off-Broadway in 2015.[6]

> "Its language is a seamless marriage of hip-hop argot and raw American history made startlingly alive."

The Public Theater is located on Lafayette Street in Manhattan's lower east side. This is perhaps appropriate, since the man after whom the street is named, Marquis de Lafayette, was a great friend of Hamilton's. But the most amazing part about this story is that before *Hamilton* had even been taken to Broadway, the show was already a smash hit. Celebrities and musicians of all genres went to see the show and sang its praises—from "Weird Al" Yankovic (the man that Miranda credits with teaching him that music could be a way to tell any story) to Sara Bareilles, Rubén Blades, Black Thought, Busta Rhymes, Jon Bon Jovi, David Byrne, Cher, Judy Collins, Josh Groban, Madonna, Jason Mraz, Q-Tip, Questlove (now a great friend of Miranda's), RZA, Regina Spektor, Swizz Beatz, and even Paul McCartney.[7] Many of these artists would go on to work with Miranda on the album "The Hamilton Mixtape."

All were excited by this new musical that blended history and legend with a contemporary sound made for the modern generation. Marilyn Stasio, theater critic for *Variety*, said after seeing the show off-Broadway,

> Although the premise sounds outlandish, it takes about two seconds to surrender to the musical sweep of the sung-through score and to Miranda's amazing vision of his towering historical subject as an ideological contemporary who reflects the thoughts and speaks the language of a vibrant young generation of immigrant strivers. It's a wonderfully humanizing view of history.[8]

The show sold out quickly, and it was clear: a hip-hop musical about Alexander Hamilton was going to Broadway.

Hamilton: An American Musical

Lin-Manuel Miranda returned to the Richard Rodgers Theatre on 46th Street. *Hamilton: An American Musical* opened for previews in July 2015. Its official opening night was on August 6, 2015. It was already the most popular show on Broadway, and it had barely

Miranda is a passionate performer, and he used that to great effect playing Alexander Hamilton. He even grew out his hair in order to make his portrayal of the founding father more authentic.

even opened. The first night, over seven hundred people lined up in hopes to win lottery tickets to see the show.[9] Miranda came out to address the crowd, "Thanks to you, we're probably going to be here a while, so don't be disappointed if you don't win today. I love you very much."[10] He didn't know just how true his words would be.

Tickets became notoriously impossible to get, not to mention difficult to afford. Not only was the show sold out months in advance but tickets could cost upward of three and four hundred dollars a seat. "Hamil-fans," as they were called, lined the sidewalks of 46th Street, hoping to get tickets for the mega hit. As the show continued in its success, Miranda wanted to make sure his musical was accessible to those who couldn't afford tickets. He gave blocks of

Javier Muñoz

Javier Muñoz is no stranger to Lin-Manuel Miranda or his work. The two have been friends since *In the Heights* in 2005. When he auditioned for a reading of that show, Muñoz had given up working in theater and had, in fact, opened the restaurant 44 ½ in Hell's Kitchen.[11] He landed the part, but it was cut from the show. However, Muñoz decided to stay on as part of the ensemble, and eventually went on to understudy for Miranda in the role of Usnavi.

Like Miranda, Muñoz grew up in a Puerto Rican family in New York City (although Muñoz grew up in Brooklyn). He studied theater at New York University. He had some minor success before *In the Heights*, but that show was his big break. On February 16, 2009, Muñoz took over for Miranda in the lead.[12] Naturally, when Miranda considered who should take over for him in the role of Alexander Hamilton, he thought of Muñoz. He had been involved with the show from the start, understudying for Miranda once again. He even began playing the role weekly.

Some wondered if the actor could handle the pressure. But Muñoz is used to stress. He was diagnosed with HIV in 2002 and has been living with the virus ever since. He was also diagnosed with cancer in October 2015. After a few weeks of chemotherapy, Muñoz was back on his feet, ready to get back to work after receiving a positive outcome.[13]

Muñoz is openly gay and is an activist who brings awareness to LGBTQ rights and HIV. Having overcome nearly as many obstacles as Alexander Hamilton, Muñoz was more than ready to take over for his friend Miranda. And with no end to the popularity of *Hamilton* in sight, that's a very good thing!

seats away to elementary students in New York City and he released the cast album on Spotify.[14] Despite the fact that the show was consistently sold out, even up to a year in advance, its popularity refuses to fade. *Hamilton*'s influences were pop culture, and now it is influencing pop culture. It is an amazing testament to the power of music and storytelling. The strangest idea for a Broadway show in centuries has become its biggest smash hit.

Countless celebrities came to see the show: politicians, journalists, television personalities, actors, musicians, and even the president and first lady.

Perhaps one of the reasons *Hamilton* is so successful is that Miranda was careful not to allow historical inaccuracies in order to tell a better story, although the story itself needs no embellishments. Aside from working with Chernow, Miranda also worked with Thomas Kail's mother, who is an archivist in Washington, DC. "She pulled up a ton of materials for me that I never would have gotten otherwise. With white gloves on, she showed me Hamilton's condolence

Miranda and the cast of *Hamilton* performed at the White House for President Barack Obama and First Lady Michelle Obama. He was honored to bring history to the White House.

letter to Martha Washington."[15]

In March 2016, Miranda, along with several other cast members, was invited to the White House to perform the smash hit for the president of the United States and his family. The day consisted of performances, a Q&A session with the press, a student workshop, and even some impromptu freestyling in the Rose Garden with the president himself.[16]

The 2016 Tony Awards

The 70th annual Tony Awards was held on June 12, 2016, at the Beacon Theater in New York City. *Hamilton* was nominated for an astonishing sixteen Tony awards. This was the largest number of Tonys ever nominated for a single Broadway show to date. James Corden, a West

End and Broadway star, as well the host of a successful late-night comedy show, hosted the program.

Lin-Manuel Miranda, Leslie Odom Jr., Daveed Diggs, Christopher Jackson, Phillipa Soo, Renée Elise Goldsberry, and the rest of the cast performed "History Has Its Eyes on You / Yorktown (The World Turned Upside Down)" from their smash hit. President and Michelle Obama introduced the performance via prerecorded video, telling the audience about their first time hearing music from *Hamilton* at the White House during its annual poetry jam seven years earlier. For many Americans who had not been fortunate enough to see the show at the Richard Rodgers Theatre, this was one of their first opportunities to see the songs performed on stage.

Hamilton won a staggering eleven Tonys that night. Leslie Odom Jr. won for Best Performance by an Actor in a Musical. Daveed Diggs won for Best Performance by a Featured Actor in a Musical. Renée Elise Goldsberry won Best Performance by a Featured Actress in a Musical for her portrayal of Angelica Schuyler-Church. *Hamilton* won for Best Book of a Musical, Best Original Score Written for Theater, Best Costume Design in a Musical, Best Lighting Design in a Musical, Best Direction of a Musical, Best Choreography, and Best Orchestrations.

MacArthur Genius Grant, the Drama League Award, and Ending *Hamilton*

In the fall of 2015, Miranda received an award he never dreamed of: a MacArthur Genius Grant. The grant is given annually to about twenty-five people whose work shows "exceptional creativity, promise for important future advances based on a track record of significant accomplishment, and potential for the fellowship to facilitate subsequent creative work."[17] It is a huge accomplishment and a great honor to receive this award. Winners are nominated for their work; they cannot apply. The award is open to any US resident for any field of work, as long as he or she does not hold elected office. Recipients include surgeons, scientists, poets, lawyers, filmmakers, historians, mathematicians, actors, directors, and musicians.

In a press release about its decision, the MacArthur Foundation said: "The daring pairing of street culture with America's founding narrative recalls the youthful, defiant spirit of the American Revolution, and cross-racial casting connects the present day to the diverse immigrant society of the thirteen rebel colonies. Melding a love of the musical with a pop culture sensibility, Miranda is expanding the conventions of mainstream theater and showcasing the cultural riches of the American urban panorama."[18] That same year, he also received an honorary doctorate from his alma mater, Wesleyan University. He also gave the commencement speech to Wesleyan graduates in the same ceremony.

On April 24, 2016, Miranda gave his final performance as Alexander Hamilton on Broadway. At the same time, Leslie Odom Jr., who played Aaron Burr; Phillipa Soo, who played Eliza Schuyler; and Daveed Diggs, who played the Marquise de Lafayette and Thomas Jefferson, also retired from the show, and Renée Elise Goldsberry,

After his final Broadway performance of Alexander Hamilton on Broadway, Miranda was moved to tears. The orchestra played the theme song from *The West Wing* while he took his final bow. Moments later, he cut off his signature long hair.

who played Eliza's sister Angelica Schuyler-Church, also left the show. It was time for a new cast to get its shot.

They promised to return "again and again."[19] Miranda said "We are aware that history has its eyes on us."[20] Minutes after the curtain closed on his final of 375 Broadway performances as Alexander Hamilton, Miranda cut off his well-known shoulder-length hair and emerged from the theater ready to take on his next adventure.

The Drama League Award celebrates individuals who accomplish outstanding achievements on Broadway and off-Broadway. It is run by the Drama League, a nonprofit organization that focuses on theater support, development, and education.[21]

It is the oldest award. Unlike the Emmys, Grammys, Oscars, and Tonys, there are only five categories. It is a great honor to be nominated. In May 2016, Lin-Manuel Miranda was given the Drama League Award for Outstanding Production of a Musical. During the same event, he received the Distinguished Performance Award. It is the oldest and most exclusive theatrical honor in North America. This award can only be received once in an actor's career.[22] It is considered one of the highest honors in theater. Past winners include Chita Rivera, Neil Patrick Harris, Nathan Lane, Audra McDonald, and many more.

Chapter Six

Disney and More

· ·

The year 2016 was a big year for the *Hamilton* star. He was now known around the world. His show was a smashing success, and many new opportunities were presenting themselves to him. Many people would consider taking a break. But not Lin-Manuel Miranda.

In January of that year, he performed in *Les Misérables* on Broadway, accomplishing a lifelong dream. *Les Misérables* was one of the many cast albums he'd grown up listening to and was the first show he saw on Broadway as a child. He wasn't, however, actually on the stage. He loaned his voice backstage as the "Loud Hailer" during a performance. The Imperial Theater, where *Les Misérables* was being presented, is directly next door to the Richard Rodgers Theatre on 46th Street. He sang twice, just a few lines. And no one in the audience knew it was happening. About the experience he said, "This is much more nerve-wracking than *Hamilton*."[1]

2016: The Year of Lin-Manuel Miranda

In April 2016, Miranda released a book called *Hamilton: The Revolution*. The book is 298 pages long and discusses

Lin-Manuel's inspiration and creation of his successful Broadway musical. The book also contains the entire script of the show and many photos, both behind-the-scenes and on the stage. It was a success as well, even being sold at the National Archives in Washington, DC. It was given a George Washington book prize, which is only awarded to exceptional books that portray the history of the United States. Shortly afterward, on May 16, Miranda received an honorary doctorate by the University of Pennsylvania.

In May 2016, Miranda gave the commencement speech for graduates of the University of Pennsylvania. He also received an honorary doctorate from the university that day.

One may not think of Lin-Manuel Miranda when thinking of the latest installment of the *Star Wars* franchise, *Star Wars: The Force Awakens*. But he composed the new original music for the "Cantina" scene. John Williams, composer for the original *Star Wars* movies, declined to write a new song to be played in the cantina. Williams, after all, had written the orchestral score for all of the films. Miranda happily stepped in. Miranda wrote the song that played in Maz Kanata's Cantina.

Moana

Also in 2016, Disney released its fifty-sixth animated feature, *Moana*. Lin-Manuel Miranda wrote the original music for the movie. The movie takes place in the Polynesian island of Motunui and follows the adventures of Moana (voiced

Miranda got to work with some of his heroes on Disney's *Moana*. He also got to make many lively press appearances and performances with Dwayne "The Rock" Johnson.

by newcomer Auli'i Cravalho); her pet chicken, Heihei; her pet pig, Pua; and the demigod Maui (voiced by Dwayne "The Rock" Johnson) who go on a journey to save her people.

Some Disney animated features, namely *Aladdin* (1992) and *Lilo and Stitch* (2002), have been criticized for not giving a true representation of their respective cultures. Because of this, Disney wanted to ensure that the music for *Moana* would be authentic and follow the traditional music of the South Pacific. They also wanted the music to be representative of Disney: Broadway-show-style numbers that reveal characters' thoughts and emotions, as well as so catchy that once heard, they become instant earworms, or songs that get stuck in a person's head. So, they turned to Broadway's biggest composer: Lin-Manuel Miranda.[2]

Along with Grammy-winning composer Mark Mancina and Samoan artist Opetaia Foa'i, Miranda studied the music of the South Pacific. Disney even sent the trio to a traditional vocal and dance festival in New Zealand! The rhythms and sounds of the music are unique to the region, and Miranda, Mancina, and Foa'i were able to create songs in both English and the Tokelauan language, native to the islands.

Miranda is known for absorbing pop culture—especially anything that contains music. His knowledge of the Disney library is astonishing. A new father, he relished in creating something that his son could enjoy as much as he did as a child. His favorite song on the soundtrack is "You're Welcome," performed by Dwayne Johnson. Of the song, Miranda said,

We did a lot of research into the different beliefs about Maui in [Polynesia], and sometimes he's responsible for pulling the sun, sometimes he's responsible for the invention of coconuts, so I loved the idea of this demigod being like, "I know it's overwhelming to meet me. You're welcome for everything."... In my head it was a mix of [the *Beauty and the Beast* song] "Gaston" and *Aladdin's* "A Friend Like Me," where the whole thing is built on Robin Williams's incredible charm."[3]

The soundtrack also utilizes traditional Polynesian songs, chants, and choirs, as well as traditional instruments such as pipes and drums.

Television Appearances

Miranda did quite a lot of press for the film. He made appearances on many late-night television shows such as *Late Night with Jimmy Fallon* and the *Late Show with Stephen Colbert*. On the *Late Late Show with James Corden*, he appeared in the show's segment "Carpool Karaoke," in which Corden, a talented singer and theater performer himself, takes his guests on a drive

> "I'm fresh off a long run performing in my musical *Hamilton*, which fortunately is one of the biggest hits ever on Broadway, which means that most of you at home have no idea who I am."

and they sing along with the radio. Miranda appeared on "Carpool Karaoke" on the week before the Tony Awards, which Corden hosted that year.

During the segment, Miranda and Corden rapped several songs from *Hamilton*. During the course of their ride through Manhattan, the pair "picked up" Audra McDonald, Jesse Tyler Ferguson, and Jane Krakowski, all members of the Broadway community who were all award-winning theater performers. Jesse Tyler Ferguson was the only person in the car who hadn't won a Tony, a fact that he freely admitted (Ferguson has won a Drama Desk Award, a Screen Actors Guild Award, and several Emmys, but as of yet, no Tony).

The group sang "Seasons of Love" from *Rent*. When the opening chords of the song began, the group let out a

In July 2016, after a devastating attack on a nightclub in Orlando, Miranda sang "Love Make the World Go Round" with Jennifer Lopez on the *Today Show*. All proceeds from sales of the song went to help the victims of the attack and their families.

collective sound of affection, proving they were not just Broadway stars but also Broadway *fans*. They also sang The Four Seasons' "Can't Take My Eyes Off of You." (The hit Broadway show *Jersey Boys* was based on the true-life story of Frankie Valli and the Four Seasons.) They ended the car ride with "One Day More" from *Les Miserables*.

Now that he was a star, Lin-Manuel Miranda was wanted everywhere. He appeared on the daytime television show *The Ellen Degeneres Show*, where he freestyle rap-improvised after the host gave him an everyday topic, using the skills he'd acquired with Freestyle Love Supreme. He also appeared on *The View*, where he danced with Whoopi Goldberg to "Footloose."

In addition, Miranda appeared on the show *Last Week Tonight with John Oliver*. The show is well-known for discussing one topic in-depth for the length of each episode. The topic that night was Puerto Rico. The island has been in economic trouble for many years. Miranda performed a freestyle rap about Puerto Rico, discussing the economic and social difficulties that plague the territory, and pleading for the United States to help the island that is just "one hundred miles across" the ocean from Florida.[4]

Also in 2016, Miranda hosted the popular sketch comedy show *Saturday Night Live* (*SNL*), fulfilling a long-time dream, since before his days in the creation of Freestyle Love Supreme. In his opening monologue, he poked fun at himself saying, "I'm fresh off a long run performing in my musical *Hamilton*, which fortunately is one of the biggest hits ever on Broadway, which means that most of you at home have no idea who I am."[5] Then, he freestyle-rapped to the tune of "My Shot" from *Hamilton* (arguably the show's most popular number). Not only did he sing and dance but he also played a substitute high school English teacher who was over-enthusiastic about inspiring his students. It was not only a nod to many films that have been about students and teachers but also to his own time teaching high school English before he became a successful Broadway star.

Lin-Manuel Miranda's Causes

Miranda gives away tickets to the most popular show on Broadway and speaks out for Puerto Rican rights. He has also helped raise money and awareness for women's rights. He helps his mother to bring awareness to the organization Planned Parenthood. Mother and son appear in many public service announcements (PSAs) on Miranda's Twitter.

Miranda also raised money for the victims and families of the Orlando night club shooting in 2016. When he received his Tony for Best Original Score, his acceptance speech was an original sonnet sixteen lines long. In it, he talked about his love for his wife, Vanessa, as well the subject of broader love and acceptance: "Love is love is love is love." The poem was inspired in part by his reaction to the Orlando shooting and also in part by a sixteen-line sonnet written by George Meredith in 1862, entitled "Modern Love."

He appeared in a Broadway tribute singing "What the World Needs Now Is Love" (originally written by Burt Bacharach) that also starred Idina Menzel, Sean

Miranda made several appearances for Hillary Clinton's 2016 presidential campaign. Here, the two pose for a photo after Clinton had seen *Hamilton* on Broadway.

Hayes, Kristen Bell, Gloria Estefan, Bernadette Peters, Carole King, Whoopi Goldberg, Matthew Broderick, and many others. All proceeds went to the LGBTQ Center of Orlando. In addition to this, he also recorded a song with Jennifer Lopez, another famous Puerto Rican New Yorker. They recorded the song "Love Make the World Go Round." All the proceeds from sales of the song went to the people affected by the night club shooting in Orlando.

He is an avid speaker for adopting pets, as opposed to buying them. He adopted his dog, Tobillo (called "Tobi" for short), from the Dominican Republic. He also helps to raise money for the Hispanic Foundation, "a non-profit organization that uplifts millions of Hispanic children, youth and families locally and nationally."[6] He

Hip Hop on (and Off) Broadway

No one can deny the influence that *Hamilton* and Lin-Manuel Miranda have had on Broadway and pop culture. Gerard Alessandrini is a musical writer for many off-Broadway shows. His most famous work, *Forbidden Broadway*, pokes satirical fun at some of Broadway's most famous shows. His most recent off-Broadway spoof is called *Spamilton: An American Parody*. It's obvious that Alessandrini admires Miranda in this parody, but still manages to poke fun at the biggest show on Broadway, as well as others such as *Cats* and *The Book of Mormon*. Miranda even saw the show and admitted he found it hilarious. He attended with Thomas Kail and Alex Lacamoire, who also enjoyed the show.

Another example of *Hamilton*'s influence on Broadway is the recent off-Broadway show *Othello: The Remix*, which is perhaps an even stranger idea than a hip-hop musical about the founding fathers. *Othello: The Remix* retells Shakespeare's famous play about a Moorish merchant who is plagued by jealousy, but with a modern hip-hop twist. The play is a "rap opera," with very little spoken dialogue. The character of Othello is no longer a merchant but instead a rapper at the height of his career, and the character of Desdemona (his wife) never appears on stage at all. Although Shakespeare's original play was far from a comedy, *Othello: The Remix* takes time to joke about itself, the modern music and entertainment industries, and even the audience. Produced by John Leguizamo, the off-Broadway show had a limited run from November 2016 through January 2017. Like *In the Heights* and *Hamilton* before it, there are talks of bringing it to Broadway.

even took a few recipients of the Hispanic Foundation's proceeds to see his last night performing in *Hamilton*.[7]

He made appearances for Hillary Clinton's 2016 presidential campaign and encouraged Americans to vote. He spoke out against Donald Trump during the 2016 campaign. Vice President Mike Pence saw *Hamilton* on Broadway on November 18, 2016. The cast of the show notoriously had a message for Pence, which was delivered during the curtain call. Miranda helped write the speech, directed at Pence to tell him how uncomfortable many of his constituents felt after the results of the incredibly divisive 2016 election. Actor Brandon Victor Dixon, who played Aaron Burr, delivered the address. Donald Trump, upon hearing of the incident, took to Twitter, saying that the behavior of the *Hamilton* cast was rude, that the event was harassment against the vice president-elect, and that theater should be a safe space. Mike Pence said, after the incident, that he wasn't offended by the address from the famously diverse cast of *Hamilton*. Miranda reiterated via Twitter that everyone was welcome in the theater.

Miranda also appeared with New York senators Kirsten Gillibrand and Charles Schumer, Massachusetts Senator Elizabeth Warren, and other Democratic lawmakers before Congress on March 16, 2016, to speak for bankruptcy protection for Puerto Rico. "This is a fixable issue," Miranda said. Puerto Rico is currently suffering from a $72 billion debt crisis and lack of jobs for its citizenry that has devastated the Puerto Rican economy.[8]

He uses his celebrity to bring awareness to his causes, helping in the only way he knows how: by using his music.

The Hamilton Mixtape and Other Recordings

In 2016, the original cast recording of *Hamilton* was nominated for a Grammy for Best Musical Theater Performance. Leslie Odom Jr., Daveed Diggs, Christopher Jackson, Renée Elise Goldsberry, Phillipa Soo, Lin-Manuel Miranda, and the rest of the cast dazzled the audience with the show's opening number,

Spamilton was a satire based on Miranda's successful Broadway show. Miranda went to see it and had a lot of fun. Because of his background in improv, comedy is something that Miranda enjoys.

the one that started it all: "Alexander Hamilton," originally called "Hamilton Mixtape." When Miranda stepped onstage, the audience roared, and the music

had to be paused before he could be heard to continue.[9] It was a moment that showed that music can transcend culture, class, race, and even genre. After the performance, Miranda and the rest of the cast won the Grammy, again to monstrous applause.

In November of that year, Miranda released the *Hamilton Mixtape*, an album that was a remix of the original music for his Broadway show. Many famous recording artists, rappers, and musicians were involved in the album. The Roots, Nas, Usher, Sia, Queen Latifah, Regina Spektor, Ben Folds, Kelly Clarkson, Ingrid Michaelson, John Legend, Chance the Rapper, and Common were just a few of the artists that Miranda worked with to create a remix of his original work. The album combines Miranda's original ideas along with the unique sounds that these artists bring to every piece of music they make. Some of the songs on the *Hamilton Mixtape* didn't make it into the Broadway show but were instead cut during the drafting and rewriting process. Others were familiar to fans of the show, such as "Wait for It," "Dear Theodosia," "It's Quiet

Uptown," "You'll Be Back," "Helpless," and arguably the show's biggest hit, "My Shot."

This excited many fans, who felt they got a more complete sense of the masterpiece that Miranda had created. Other fans were excited to see Miranda collaborate with some of his heroes like Busta Rhymes, Wiz Khalifa, and Alicia Keys. Others, eager for more *Hamilton*, were simply excited to hear a new take on some of their favorite songs. The album was an immediate hit and immediately shot to the top of the *Billboard 100* list, an accomplishment that hadn't been done by a compilation album in over two years.

A month later, Penguin Audio released an unabridged audiobook for the novel *The Brief Wondrous Life of Oscar Wao*, written by Junot Díaz. The book runs for nine hours and fifty-three minutes and stars Lin-Manuel Miranda and Karen Olivo. Olivo is another well-known Broadway star, having won a Tony for her performance of "Anita" in the Broadway revival of *West Wide Story*. She is also starring as Eliza Schuyler-Hamilton in the production of *Hamilton* that opened in Chicago.

> **"When Miranda stepped on stage, the audience roared, and the music had to be paused before he could be heard to continue."**

Hardly a day passed in 2016 when Lin-Manuel Miranda wasn't in the news. Whether it was for his work in *Hamilton*, his charity work, his encouragement of voters, his meetings with dignitaries, or his multiple television appearances, by the end of 2016, hardly a person in the United States didn't know who he was. Much like his character in *Hamilton*, Miranda seemed able to write like he was "running out of time."

A special episode of the PBS documentary film series *Great Performances* was made about Miranda and *Hamilton*. *Hamilton's America: A Documentary Film* follows Miranda from his early days while writing and workshopping *Hamilton* all the way through its run on Broadway. During the several years that it covers, much had changed for Miranda. His idea became a full Broadway musical, with his dream cast of collaborators and performers. He became a father. He became one of the biggest stars in the world. The political climate of America had changed, along with the way it needed to be represented. The documentary also chronicled the life of Alexander Hamilton, in which Miranda got to interview historians about the man who had inspired his most famous character. It premiered on PBS on October 21, 2016.

The Associated Press named him Entertainer of the Year.[10] He was far more than one of Broadway's biggest stars. He was one of the biggest stars in the world.[11]

CHAPTER SEVEN

"What Comes Next?"

• •

There is no doubt that *Hamilton* is one of the most popular Broadway shows in history. And Lin-Manuel Miranda has had more opportunities because of it. Not only has he worked with Disney, which is a lifelong dream, but he is now friends and collaborators with some of the people he's long admired. He can call Questlove when he wants to write a song, or Stephen Sondheim when he has a new idea for a play. And as the star left *Hamilton*, it seemed that everyone wanted to work with him. And Miranda relished the opportunity.

Disney's Biggest Fan

Lin-Manuel Miranda makes no secret that he is a big fan of Disney. As with most Americans his age, he grew up on Disney classics like *Cinderella* (1950), *Sleeping Beauty* (1954), *The Jungle Book* (1967), *Robin Hood* (1973), and then later *The Little Mermaid* (1989), *Beauty and the Beast* (1991), and *Aladdin* (1992). And he's never denied that fact. "My God, those Disney

Many celebrities went to see *Hamilton*. Actors, musicians, politicians, and sports stars all loved the musical. Here, Miranda poses with New York Yankees icon Derek Jeter after a performance.

musicals. I feel really lucky that I was a kid when they went on that run of animated musicals, starting with *The Little Mermaid*. Not just animated movies, animated musicals."[1] He even named his son Sebastian after the Jamaican crab in *The Little Mermaid*.[2]

> **"I feel really lucky that I was a kid when [Disney] went on that run of animated musicals, starting with *The Little Mermaid.*"**

As he began his partnership with Disney in 2015, he started to post videos on Twitter of himself singing famous Disney songs.[3] While promoting *Moana* in 2016, Miranda took over Disney's official Instagram page and posted videos of himself singing such classics as "Gaston" from *Beauty and the Beast*, "One Jump Ahead" from *Aladdin*, and "I'll Make a Man Out of You" from *Mulan*, much to both Miranda and Disney fans' delight.[4]

Mary Poppins

In early 2016, Disney announced plans to reboot the classic 1964 film *Mary Poppins*, which starred Julie Andrews and Dick Van Dyke. Fans of the film were dubious at first, worried that a reboot would tarnish the reputation of the classic film that follows the Banks family and their magical nanny in London. But soon after the project was announced, it was revealed that actress Emily Blunt would play the iconic role of Mary Poppins, and Lin-Manuel Miranda would play Jack, a lamplighter friend of Mary's who helps the now-grown Banks children through a personal loss.[5]

In the original film, Mary Poppins's friend Bert was a chimney sweep played by Dick Van Dyke. Van Dyke was well-known in the entertainment industry at the time, having starred in television and on Broadway (he had starred in *Bye Bye Birdie* and *The Music Man*). Van Dyke had also had his own television show, *The Dick Van Dyke Show*, and was known for his ability to perform flawless physical comedy.

Miranda seems a perfect fit to replace Van Dyke in a twenty-first-century adaptation of *Mary Poppins*. Disney has made it perfectly clear that the film will not be a remake. Instead, the film will take place twenty years after the original film, and is intended for fans of the original, but also intended to introduce a new audience to the story.[6] The film will also reportedly star Ben Whishaw, a well-known West End and Broadway

In 2016, Lin-Manuel Miranda was honored to receive a star on the Puerto Rican walk of fame in San Juan.

actor, and Julie Andrews and Dick Van Dyke have both suggested they may make appearances in the film, which is slated to open in December 2018.[7]

The Little Mermaid

But Disney wasn't done with Miranda yet. In August 2016, Disney announced it was planning on continuing its trend of remaking its classic animated films into live-action features. Having found success with *Cinderella* in 2015 and *The Jungle Book* in 2016, and the much-hyped released of *Beauty and the Beast* in 2017, Disney decided the next classic animated film to get the live-action treatment would be one of its most successful animated films: *The Little Mermaid*.[8]

Alan Menken was the composer of the original music for Disney's *The Little Mermaid*. Iconic songs such as "Under the Sea," "Kiss the Girl," and "Part of Your World," have become well-known to Disney fans. The children who watched the film when it was first released are grown up now, having children of their own and introducing a whole new generation to Disney. Miranda is just one of those grown-up children. And in 2016, he got a dream opportunity he couldn't pass up: to work with Menken to create the soundtrack for the newest Disney live-action film.[9]

But perhaps the most exciting thing about Disney's *The Little Mermaid* live-action film is that it will incorporate some of the classic songs that made it iconic, combined with new songs of Menken and Miranda's composing. Fans and critics alike can't wait to see how the new music stays true to its roots,

EGOT, PEGOT, and MacPEGOT

Emmy, Grammy, Oscar (Academy Award), Tony—these are the biggest awards given in the entertainment industry. An artist who has collected all of these awards is instantly elevated to super celebrity status. Not only are the individuals tremendously talented but they are household names. Artists who have been elevated to this status include Richard Rodgers (of Rodgers and Hammerstein), Audrey Hepburn (*Breakfast at Tiffany's, Roman Holiday*), Marvin Hamlisch (a well-known musical composer for film and television), Mel Brooks (*Young Frankenstein, The Producers*), Whoopi Goldberg, Barbra Streisand, Liza Minelli, and James Earl Jones.

PEGOT winners have one more award to their names—the Peabody Award. Richard Rodgers, Barbra Streisand, and Marvin Hamlisch have been elevated to this status, but few others have.[10]

Since winning the Pulitzer Prize and the MacArthur Genius grant, there is a new acronym floating around the entertainment industry concerning Miranda—MacPEGOT. MacArthur Genius Grant, Emmy, Grammy, Oscar, and Tony.

Miranda won the MacArthur Genius award in 2015. He won a Pulitzer Prize in 2016. In 2014, he was awarded a Primetime Emmy for his work on the song "Bigger" (with Tom Kitt) for the 67th Tony Awards. He won a Grammy with the soundtrack of *Hamilton* in 2016. And he's been winning Tonys (Antoinette Perry Award for Excellence in Theater) since 2008.

All that Lin-Manuel Miranda is missing is the O—an Oscar (Academy Award). And that, it seems, is likely to happen very soon.[11]

while also breathing new life into the story. The film will star Chloë Grace Moretz as Ariel, and, as of this writing, is still in preproduction, which means the script, music, casting, and shooting details are still being worked out. But Disney fans are excited to see the film and are thrilled that Broadway's biggest star, Disney's newest darling, and possibly his generation's greatest songwriter will be involved. And Miranda is a huge fan of the original. He proudly proclaims that it is his favorite Disney movie. "I don't know why it changed my life as much as it did. I think Sebastian the crab had a big amount to do with it—the fact that this calypso number happens under the water just knocked my socks off when I was a kid. It had this power over me. I would perform that thing—I would jump up on my desk in fourth grade and sing that song."[12]

Film Producer

Even with several projects in the works, Lin-Manuel Miranda didn't show any signs of stopping. In the fall of 2016, he announced that he would be adding "film producer" to the ever-growing list of roles he plays in the entertainment industry.

Lionsgate decided to make a film adaptation of the popular fantasy trilogy *The Kingkiller Chronicle*, hoping for the film to lead to a television series. The books were written by Pat Rothfuss, and follow the adventures of master sword fighter, magician, and musician Kvothe. Miranda is slated to write the music for the film, as well as to help produce it.[13] The film will follow the first book in the trilogy *The Name of the Wind*, while the television show will delve beyond the original books. Miranda and Rothfuss will create new characters and storylines for the show.[14]

Miranda is a big fan of the series. He has admitted that the *Hamilton* song "The Story of Tonight" was inspired by a scene in the book.[15] There are also options for a future stage adaptation of the books, of which, naturally, Miranda is considering.[16] Music plays a very important role in the books, and both Miranda and Rothfuss wanted to make sure the film, television show, and possible stage adaptations reflected that. Inspired by medieval music, Miranda has begun working on the project with a lute. In a tweet from November 29, 2016, Miranda said: "*stares at a lute for 20 minutes, sweats profusely* Okay, so we're doing this. @PatrickRothfuss."[17] This may seem like a departure from Miranda's usual Broadway, pop, and hip-hop. But considering he has a musical education, and that he studied the traditional music of the South Pacific for Moana, it doesn't really seem like that much of a stretch for his talents and capabilities.

Making Broadway Available for Everyone

Although ticket sales for *Hamilton* don't appear to be slowing any time soon, it is known for also being one of the most expensive shows on Broadway. Tickets for Broadway shows can cost several hundred dollars. But tickets for *Hamilton* have been priced in the thousands. This, of course, makes it impossible to see the show for many people. Miranda, as well as many other performers, blame ticketbots for this. Ticketbots are computer programs that purchase tickets in bulk and then resell them at a much higher cost. Ticketbots are illegal, but nonetheless they prevail in selling tickets for concerts, Broadway shows, and many other live events. The people who run these programs can make a lot of money reselling their tickets at five or ten times the original cost.

Lin-Manuel Miranda knows his show is a success, but he wants it to be available to everyone. That's the reason Miranda made the soundtrack for *Hamilton* (as well as the *Hamilton Mixtape*), available on Spotify, a music-playing platform that allows listeners to hear whole albums. Many artists don't release their albums on Spotify and its free counterparts in order to raise their album sales.

Miranda joined forces with New York senator Chuck Schumer in order to try and stop ticketbots. An investigation in 2015 revealed that ticketbots are making tickets almost impossible to obtain. "Tens of thousands of tickets to New York events are acquired each year using such software. Brokers who buy tickets using bots substantially mark up the prices— sometimes by more than 1,000 percent—yielding enormous profits," Miranda said in an opinion piece he wrote for the *New York Times* in 2016.[18] It is illegal to use ticketbots, but somehow, they are still involved in getting tickets for concerts and Broadway shows.

Along with Schumer, Miranda wants to stop ticketbots from making tickets too expensive for the average theatergoer. "My concern is that our show is about the founding of our country and if bots are buying up all the tickets and charging this insane secondary market price, most of the country can't see it," Miranda said in a press conference with Schumer in August 2016.[19]

The average *Hamilton* ticket costs between $250 and $900 (for premium seats). There is a lottery to win $10 tickets to performances the day of, a "Hamilton" for *Hamilton*. Lottery participants enter online or at the box office. Winners are selected at random. They are able to enter the lottery for evening performances at 9 a.m. (eastern standard time), and winners are announced at 4 p.m. For matinees, participants can enter at 9 a.m., and winners are announced at noon. On those days, there is another lottery for tickets to the evening performance beginning at noon, with winners being announced at 4 p.m. Twenty-one tickets are reserved for lottery winners for each performance of *Hamilton*. But it is estimated that something like 10,000 people enter the online lottery for every performance, so the odds of winning tickets are low.[20]

However, Miranda created a hashtag for this lottery, and his hope is that everyone who wants to see his musical can. #Ham4Ham uses social media to promote the lottery and Miranda's desire to make theater accessible to everyone. He uses various social media platforms to show videos, photos, and messages from *Hamilton* fans and himself. When he was still performing in the show, Miranda would appear outside the stage door and give impromptu performances for (and sometimes with) fans. He would also post videos (such as the backstage footage of himself performing in *Les Miserables*) that promoted theater in general.[21] Often, other stars of the show, such as Jonathan Groff,

The #Ham4Ham performances were a viral sensation. Miranda's performances at the stage door promoted the lottery for tickets and allowed him to meet his fans.

the cast of *In the Heights*, and many others would appear in the videos. Fans posted their own performances with the hashtag #Ham4Ham as well.

Miranda is adamant, however, that ticketbots continue to be a problem for ticker buyers. "I want the thousands of tickets for shows, concerts and sporting events that are now purchased by bots and resold at higher prices to go into the general market so that you have a chance to get them. I want theatergoers to be able to purchase tickets at face value at our box office and our website, rather than on a resale platform. And if you do go to a resale platform for tickets, I want the markup you must pay to be clearly displayed. Most of all, I want you to be there when the curtain goes up. You shouldn't have to fight robots just to see something you love."[22]

A Social Media Darling

Miranda is very active on social media. Not only has he created hashtags but he also has tens of thousands of followers on Tumblr, Twitter, and Facebook. And he uses these platforms in a fun, entertaining way. He talks about his upcoming projects, gives shout-outs to people who inspired him, and gives thanks to fans. He posts videos of himself both today and as a child or a teenager: performing, speaking, rapping, or singing. When he took over the official Disney Instagram in 2016 and sang Disney songs, they immediately went viral and were reposted everywhere.[23] He snapped a photo with Ron Clements and John Musker and captioned it: "This is Ron & John. They directed *The Little Mermaid*, the first movie that made me want to spend my life making music. They also directed *Moana*. I got to make music for them. Dreams come true, kids. This is proof."[24]

He has well over one million followers on Twitter, the social media platform he uses most. He posts daily about his everyday life, which, to his fans, is fascinating. He has nearly that many on Tumblr. Many of the videos and photos he posts are funny and show that Miranda has a warm, light-hearted personality that is perfect for the entertainment industry.

In addition to using the traditional social media platforms and his numerous television appearances, Miranda has also appeared on the podcast *My Brother, My Brother, and Me*. Miranda is a fan of the podcast, which is hosted by brothers Justin, Travis, and Griffin McElroy. The comedy podcast features the brothers hilariously answering questions either posited to the hosts themselves or found on Yahoo! answers. The show often has guests, called "guestperts" by the McElroy brothers. Miranda appeared to discuss musical theater, and featured "it has three part harmonies about ghost horses."[25]

In January 2017, Miranda appeared on National Public Radio's *Fresh Air*. The radio show is broadcast five days a week and has an estimated five million listeners. The show has been on the air for over forty years and features many interviews with experts in their fields, from news to history, to arts and entertainment. Miranda talked candidly about his childhood, his education, and his experiences on Broadway. When asked if he thought he could top *Hamilton*, Miranda said,

> "If you think in terms of topping, you're in the wrong business ... I went from broke substitute teacher to Broadway composer. I will never make a leap that big in my life again."

> If you think in terms of topping, you're in the wrong business. I remember getting that question after *In the Heights*. "It's your first musical and you won the Tony, how are you going to top it?" I'm like, "I went from broke substitute teacher to Broadway composer. I will never make a leap that big in my life again."[26]

And He's Still Not Done

With all the projects on the horizon for Lin-Manuel Miranda, it is clear that he's not leaving the public eye any time soon. In 2016, he started living in London to begin filming *Mary Poppins*. But he keeps his apartment in Washington Heights, wishing to keep in touch with his family and his roots. "I love New York like you love your grandparents. If you grow up in New York City and you're paying attention, you have a better spidey sense than anyone else. It prepares you well for the rest of the world. You learn to listen to the hair on the back of your neck."[27] Still active on social media and writing music, it seems like there is no stopping Miranda. He no longer just admires pop culture—he creates and inspires it.

He has another animated film, *Vivo*, slotted to be released by Sony Pictures Animation in December 2020. The film's screenplay will be written by Miranda's collaborator on *In the Heights*, Quiara Alegría Hudes. The film will feature eleven songs, already written by Miranda.[28]

There is also an *In the Heights* movie being made. There had originally been talks for a film adaptation back in 2008 when it was on Broadway, but it was put aside by the film studios. However, with the success of *Hamilton*, *Moana*, and Miranda's many other projects, the film is finally being made, and is in preproduction. The script is being written by Hudes, and Miranda will be in the film. He will not reprise his role as Usnavi, however. Instead, he will either represent another character from the play or a new character written exclusively for the film.

On December 12, 2016, his song "How Far I'll Go" for *Moana* was nominated for a Golden Globe.

Lin-Manuel Miranda is one of the best-known stars of Broadway. And his star continues to rise. With films, television, and other projects on the horizon, Miranda will continue to influence the entertainment industry for years to come.

Miranda announced it to the world by tweeting: "Bit of a day, bit of a day, bit of a day!"[29] Although he didn't win, another musical swept the show. *La La Land* (2016), a movie musical about a struggling jazz pianist in Los Angeles, won a record-breaking seven awards that night. Although Miranda didn't win, it's clear that he's made an impact on American pop culture.

Musicals are suddenly, once again, all the rage. And it's in large part because Lin-Manuel Miranda brought them to the forefront of everyone's minds, and has made them relatable to the average person. *Hamilton* brought theater into the twenty-first century. It wasn't just in a theater. It was on television, on the internet, on social media, and even in the White House. The theater was once again a topic of everyday conversation. At a time when the Internet, television, smartphones, and movies are widely available, Miranda has inspired people to go and see live theater and to want to hear stories that are sung (or rapped) to the music of the times.

So, what else is next for Miranda? He freely admits he has his eye on directing a big movie musical.[30] Could it be *Hamilton*? Or could it be one of the classics he grew up hearing at home? He admits he always has ideas, "*Hamilton*-size ideas."[31] There are even rumors of a "secret project" with Disney.

Miranda can no longer walk down the streets of New York (or many other places) without being stopped by fans. He remains humble and stops to chat with them, take selfies with them, and sign autographs. His success has skyrocketed him to superstardom, and yet, he still appreciates his fans. He remembers where he came from, that he was once just like them: a fan of music, theater, and Broadway.

As one journalist put it, in an ode to Miranda's achievements, "The significance of *Hamilton* is more than the play itself; Miranda got an entire country, often apathetic to the arts, to care about musical theater. It is rare that a single thing, whether it's a book, movie, or play, has such an impact."[32] Lin-Manuel Miranda has devoted his life to the theater, to music, and to creating art. His passion is to share his creations with the world, and with an impressive catalog of work already behind him, it is clear that this is just the beginning.

Chronology

January 16, 1980 Lin-Manuel Miranda is born in Washington Heights, New York City.

1998 Miranda graduates from Hunter College High School and begins attending Wesleyan University, where he meets Christopher Jackson.

1999 Miranda begins writing the first draft of *In the Heights* and helps to form Freestyle Love Supreme; puts on first production of *In the Heights* at Wesleyan, where he meets Thomas Kail, Anthony Veneziale, John Buffalo Mailer, and Neil Stewart.

2002 Graduates from Wesleyan University.

2003–2005 Miranda begins workshopping *In the Heights.*

2005 *In the Heights* performed off-Broadway, in Connecticut's Eugene O'Neill Theatre for the National Theatre Conference.

2008 **February 8** *In the Heights* opens on Broadway at the Richard Rodgers Theatre; **June 15** Miranda wins four Tonys for *In the Heights*, for Best Musical, Best Original Score, Best

Orchestrations, and Best Choreography; reads Ron Chernow's *Alexander Hamilton* and begins drafting the first songs for *Hamilton.*

2009 February 9 Miranda and cast of *In the Heights* win a Grammy for Best Musical Show; gets honorary degree from Yeshiva University; performs a piece from the "Hamilton Mixtape" at the White House Poetry Jam.

2010 Lin-Manuel Miranda marries Vanessa Nadal.

2011 Cowrites music and lyrics for *Bring It On: The Musical.*

2012 Appears in *Modern Family, How I Met Your Mother, The Odd Life of Timothy Green*; performs sections of the "Hamilton Mixtape" at the Allen Room in New York City .

2013 Has a reoccurring role in *Do No Harm.*

2014 Appears in *21 Chump Street* for *This American Life*; **November 10** Son Sebastian is born.

2015 **January** *Hamilton* begins being performed off-Broadway at the Public Theatre in New York City; **July** *Hamilton* opens at the Richard Rodgers Theatre and is instantly the hottest show on Broadway; wins MacArthur Genius Grant; receives honorary doctorate from Wesleyan University.

2016 Performs behind the scenes in *Les Miserables* on Broadway; the cast of *Hamilton* performs at the White House; **June 12** *Hamilton* wins eleven out of its record-breaking sixteen nominations at the Tonys; gives final (375th) performance of Alexander Hamilton on Broadway; releases *Hamilton: The Revolution*; wins Drama League Distinguished Performance Award; wins Pulitzer Prize; receives honorary doctorate from the University of Pennsylvania and from Wesleyan College; composes "Cantina Song" for *Star Wars: The Force Awakens*; appears on *Late Night with Jimmy Fallon, The Late Late Show with James Corden, Last Week Tonight with John Oliver,* and *The Ellen Degeneres Show*; helps with Hillary Clinton campaign and encourages Americans to vote; hosts *Saturday Night Live*; helps compose music and lyrics for Disney's *Moana*; wins Grammy for Best Musical Performance for *Hamilton*; appears in the PBS special episode of *Great Performances* called *Hamilton's America: A Documentary*; releases *The Hamilton Mixtape*, which remixes some of his songs from *Hamilton* with pop, hip-hop, and rap recording artists; records audiobook for *The Brief Wondrous Life of Oscar Wao*; awarded AP's Entertainer of the Year; is announced to be part of Disney's reboot of *Mary Poppins*; begins working with Alan Menken to write new music for Disney's live-action *The Little Mermaid*; begins working with Pat Rothfuss to produce *The Kingkiller Chronicle* as film and television series; writes opinion pieces for the *New York Times*, promoting Senator Chuck Shumer's legislation to keep ticketbots from making Broadway tickets more expensive; nominated for a Golden Globe for his work on *Moana*; announces animated film with Sony Animation, *Vivo*.

2017 Appears on NPR's *Fresh Air*; begins working on *Mary Poppins* in London; nominated for an Academy Award for his work on *Moana*.

Chapter Notes

Chapter 1: A Star is Born

1. National Endowment for the Arts, *Lin-Manuel Miranda: Immigrant Songs.* https://www.arts.gov/ NEARTS/2016v1-telling-all-our-stories-arts-and-diversity/lin-manuel-miranda

2. Michael Paulson, "Lin-Manuel Miranda, Creator and Star of 'Hamilton' Grew Up on Hip-Hop and Show Tunes," *The New York Times*, August 12, 2015. http://www.nytimes.com/2015/08/16/theater/lin-manuel-miranda-creator-and-star-of-hamilton-grew-up-on-hip-hop-and-show-tunes.html?_r=0

3. Michael Gioia, "Where It All Began-A Conversation With Lin-Manuel Miranda and His Father." *Playbill. com* http://www.playbill.com/article/where-it-all-begana-conversation-with-lin-manuel-miranda-and-his-father-com-353054

4. Carolina Moreno, "Lin-Manuel Miranda's Mom Shares Anecdoes of Little Lin at 'Hamilton' Farewell," *Huffington Post*, July 10, 2016, http://www.huffingtonpost.com/entry/lin-manuel-miranda-mother-hamilton-farewell_us_578270b1e4b0c590f7e9cba8

5. Lin-Manuel Miranda, "Scaling the Heights", Broadway. com http://www.broadway.com/buzz/6213/lin-manuel-miranda-scaling-the-heights/

6. Stephen Raskauskas "Lin-Manuel Miranda: 'An Arts Education… Saved My Life,'" WFMT.com http://www.wfmt.com/2016/10/07/lin-manuel-miranda-arts-educationsaved-life/

7. Ibid.

8. Ibid.

Chapter 2: Wesleyan Years

1. Michael Paulson, "Lin-Manuel Miranda, Creator and Star of 'Hamilton' Grew Up on Hip-Hop and Show Tunes," *The New York Times*, August 12, 2015. http://www.nytimes.com/2015/08/16/theater/lin-manuel-miranda-creator-and-star-of-hamilton-grew-up-on-hip-hop-and-show-tunes.html?_r=0

2. Jeff MacGregor, "Meet Lin-Manuel Miranda, the Genius Behind 'Hamilton,' Broadway's Newest Hit". *Smithsonian Magazine*, November 12, 2015, http://www.smithsonianmag.com/arts-culture/lin-manuel-miranda-ingenuity-awards-180957234/?no-ist

3. Billboard Staff, "Lin-Manuel Miranda Stars in New Show 'Freestyle Love Supreme'. *Billboard Magazine*, June 10, 2016, http://www.billboard.com/articles/news/7401071/lin-manuel-miranda-stars-freestyle-love-supreme-exclusive-clip

4. Ernio Hernandez, "New York-Set, Hip-Hop-Salsa-Merengue Musical *In the Heights* Starts at O'Neill Center, July 23" *Playbill.com*, July 23, 2005, http://www.playbill.com/article/new-york-set-hip-hop-salsa-merengue-musical-in-the-heights-starts-at-oneill-center-july-23-com-127114

5. Lin-Manuel Miranda, "Scaling the Heights", Broadway. com http://www.broadway.com/buzz/6213/lin-manuel-miranda-scaling-the-heights/

Chapter 3: *In the Heights*

1. Michael Paulson, "Lin-Manuel Miranda, Creator and Star of 'Hamilton' Grew Up on Hip-Hop and Show Tunes," *The New York Times*, August 12, 2015. http://www.nytimes.com/2015/08/16/theater/lin-manuel-miranda-creator-and-star-of-hamilton-grew-up-on-hip-hop-and-show-tunes.html?_r=0

2. National Endowment for the Arts, *Lin-Manuel Miranda: Immigrant Songs.* https://www.arts.gov/NEARTS/2016v1-telling-all-our-stories-arts-and-diversity/lin-manuel-miranda

3. Thom Geier "15 Top-Grossing Broadway Musicals of All Time", *Thewrap.com*, http://www.thewrap.com/15-top-grossing-broadway-shows-hairspray-lion-king/21/

4. National Endowment for the Arts, *Lin-Manuel Miranda: Immigrant Songs.* https://www.arts.gov/NEARTS/2016v1-telling-all-our-stories-arts-and-diversity/lin-manuel-miranda

5. Ernio Hernandez, "New York-Set, Hip-Hop-Salsa-Merengue Musical *In the Heights* Starts at O'Neill Center, July 23" *Playbill.com*, July 23, 2005, http://www.playbill.com/article/new-york-set-hip-hop-salsa-merengue-musical-in-the-heights-starts-at-oneill-center-july-23-com-127114

6. National Endowment for the Arts, *Lin-Manuel Miranda: Immigrant Songs*. https://www.arts.gov/NEARTS/2016v1-telling-all-our-stories-arts-and-diversity/lin-manuel-miranda

Chapter 4: "My Shot": More Music Making

1. Lois Smith Brady, Vanessa Nadal and Lin-Manuel Miranda, *The New York Times*, September 10, 2010, http://www.nytimes.com/2010/09/12/fashion/weddings/12VOWS.html

2. Ibid.

3. Megan French, "Lin-Manuel Miranda's Wife, Vanessa Nadal: Five Things You Should Know!" *Us Magazine*, June 13, 2016, http://www.usmagazine.com/celebrity-news/news/lin-manuel-mirandas-wife-vanessa-nadal-five-things-to-know-w209933

4. Tom Stoeklker, "Law Alumna Gives Backstage Scoop on Hamilton", *Fordham News*, October 30, 2015, http://news.fordham.edu/arts-and-culture/law-alumna-gives-backstage-scoop-on-hamilton/

5. Lois Smith Brady, Vanessa Nadal and Lin-Manuel Miranda, *The New York Times*, September 10, 2010, http://www.nytimes.com/2010/09/12/fashion/weddings/12VOWS.html

6. Jeff MacGregor, "Meet Lin-Manuel Miranda, the Genius Behind 'Hamilton,' Broadway's Newest Hit". *Smithsonian Magazine*, November 12, 2015, http://www.smithsonianmag.com/arts-culture/lin-manuel-miranda-ingenuity-awards-180957234/?no-ist

7. "'Hamilton' creator performs 'Mixtape' at 2009 White House Poetry Jam", *The Washington Post*, March 15, 2016, https://www.washingtonpost.com/video/national/lin-manuel-miranda-performs-at-the-2009-white-house-poetry-jam/2016/03/15/b56a941a-ea82-11e5-a9ce-681055c7a05f_video.html

8. "'Hamilton' wins 11 Tony Awards on a night that balances sympathy with perseverance", *The Los Angeles Times*, June 13, 2016, http://www.latimes.com/entertainment/la-et-cm-tony-awards-live-updates-hamilton-at-the-white-house-then-and-1465612652-htmlstory.html

Chapter 5: *Hamilton*

1. National Endowment for the Arts, *Lin-Manuel Miranda: Immigrant Songs.* https://www.arts.gov/NEARTS/2016v1-telling-all-our-stories-arts-and-diversity/lin-manuel-miranda

2. Jeff MacGregor, "Meet Lin-Manuel Miranda, the Genius Behind 'Hamilton,' Broadway's Newest Hit". *Smithsonian Magazine*, November 12, 2015, http://www.smithsonianmag.com/arts-culture/lin-manuel-miranda-ingenuity-awards-180957234/?no-ist

3. Ibid.

4. Stephen Holden, "Putting the Hip-Hop in History as Founding Fathers Rap". *The New York Times*, January 12, 2012, http://www.nytimes.com/2012/01/13/arts/music/hamilton-mixtape-by-lin-manuel-miranda-at-allen-room.html

5. Ibid.

6. Adam Hetrick, "Lin-Manuel Miranda's *Hamilton* to Be Stages at the Public Theater", *Playbill.com*, March 6, 2014, http://www.playbill.com/article/lin-manuel-mirandas-hamilton-to-be-staged-at-the-public-theater-com-215713

7. Michael Paulson, "Lin-Manuel Miranda, Creator and Star of 'Hamilton' Grew Up on Hip-Hop and Show Tunes," *The New York Times*, August 12, 2015. http://www.nytimes.com/2015/08/16/theater/lin-manuel-miranda-creator-and-star-of-hamilton-grew-up-on-hip-hop-and-show-tunes.html?_r=0

8. Marilyn Stasio, "Off Broadway Review: Hamilton by Lin-Manuel Miranda", *Variety.com* February 17, 2015, http://variety.com/2015/legit/reviews/review-hamilton-public-theater-lin-manuel-miranda-1201435257/

9. Michael Gioia, "Hundreds Mob the First *Hamilton* Lottery- See Which Broadway Star won!" *Playbill.com*, July 14, 2015, http://www.playbill.com/article/hundreds-mob-the-first-hamilton-lottery-see-which-broadway-star-won-com-353241

10. Ibid.

11. Carey Purcell, "Meet *Hamilton*'s Other Leading Man, Standing By Lin-Manuel Miranda for More Than Ten Years," *Playbill.com*, August 10, 2015, http://www.playbill.com/article/meet-hamiltons-other-leading-man-standing-by-for-lin-manuel-miranda-for-more-than-ten-years-com-356678

12. Dan Avery "The New Star of 'Hamilton' is Gay, HIV-Positive and Faced Down Cancer. Broadway Should

Be A Snap", *Newnownex.com*, July 11, 2016, http://
www.newnownext.com/the-new-star-of-hamilton-is-
gay-hiv-positive-and-faced-down-cancer-broadway-
should-be-a-snap/07/2016/

13. Rebecca Milzoff, "Lin-Manuel Miranda on Jay-Z,
    The West Wing, and 18 More Things That Influenced
    Hamilton", *Vulture.com*, January 15, 2016, http://
    www.vulture.com/2015/07/lin-manuel-mirandas-20-
    hamilton-influences.html

14. Michael Paulson, "Students Will Get Tickets to
    'Hamilton' With Its Hip-Hop-Infused History", *The
    New York Times*, October 27, 2015, http://www.
    nytimes.com/2015/10/27/theater/students-will-get-
    tickets-to-hamilton-with-its-hip-hop-infused-history.
    html

15. Jackie Calmes, "Harriet Tubman Ousts Andrew
    Jackson in Change for a $20", *The New York Times*,
    April 20, 2016, http://www.nytimes.com/2016/04/21/
    us/women-currency-treasury-harriet-tubman.html?_
    r=0

16. Anastasia Tsioulcas, "'Hamilton' Freestyles
    At the White House. Mic. Drop.", *NPR.org*,
    March 15, 2016, http://www.npr.org/sections/
    therecord/2016/03/15/470515719/hamilton-freestyles-
    at-the-white-house-mic-drop

17. MacArthur Foundation, *MacArthur Fellows*, ©
    2017, https://www.macfound.org/programs/fellows/
    strategy/

18. MacArthur Foundation, *Lin-Manuel Miranda: Playwright, Composer, and Performer*, September 28, 2015, https://www.macfound.org/fellows/941/

19. Mark Kennedy, "Lin-Manuel Miranda leaving 'Hamilton' July 9, vows to return" *AP.org*, June 16, 2016, http://bigstory.ap.org/article/377ef8b2fbe34 ea4ad54838223cf5230/lin-manuel-miranda-leave-hamilton-july-9

20. Ibid.

21. Gordon Cox, "'Hamilton,' 'The Humans' Win 2016 Drama League Awards" *Variety.com*, May 20, 2016, http://variety.com/2016/legit/news/2016-drama-league-awards-full-list-hamilton-1201779639/

22. The Drama League, *Award History*, DramaLeague.org, http://dramaleague.org/events/awards/award-history#%E2%80%8BDistinguished%20Performance%20Award

Chapter 6: Disney and More

1. Robert Viagas, "Lin-Manuel Miranda Debuts in *Les Miserables* in New Ham4Ham", *Playbill.com*, January 27, 2016, http://www.playbill.com/article/lin-manuel-miranda-debuts-in-les-miserables-in-new-ham4ham-com-382550

2. Melinda Newman, "Lin-Manuel Miranda, Mark Mancina & Opetaia Foa'I on Creating Disney's 'Moana,'" *Billboard.com*, November 23, 2016, http://www.billboard.com/articles/news/7588008/lin-manuel-miranda-mark-mancina-opetaia-foai-disney-moana-music

3. Ibid.

4. Ryan Reid, "John Oliver Enlists 'Hamilton' Creator to Rap About Puerto Rico Crisis", *Rollingstone.com*, April 25, 2016, http://www.rollingstone.com/tv/news/john-oliver-enlists-hamilton-creator-to-rap-about-puerto-rico-crisis-20160425

5. PR Newswire, "Lin-Manuel Miranda Raises 2 Million Dollars For Charity Through Charity Network" July 7, 2016, http://www.prnewswire.com/news-releases/lin-manuel-miranda-raises-2-million-dollars-for-charity-through-charity-network-fundraising-platforms-300294815.html

6. Ibid.

7. Daniel Macht, "'Hamilton's' Lin-Manuel Miranda Calls for Action on Puerto Rico's Debt Crisis", *NBCnewyork.com*, March 14, 2016,http://www.nbcnewyork.com/news/national-international/Hamiltons-Lin-Manuel-Miranda-Talks-Puerto-Rico-Debt-Crisis-372110872.html

8. Playbill Staff, "Watch Lin-Manuel Miranda's Top *Saturday Night Live* Sketches", *Playbill.com* October 9, 2016, http://www.playbill.com/article/watch-lin-manuel-mirandas-saturday-night-live-sketches

9. Matt Wilstein, "Watch the 'Hamilton' Cast Blow the Roof Off the Grammys", *TheDailyBeast.com*, February 15, 2016, http://www.thedailybeast.com/articles/2016/02/15/watch-the-hamilton-cast-blow-the-roof-off-the-grammys.html

10. Mark Kennedy, "2016 Year IN Review: Lin-Manuel Miranda named AP Entertainer of the

year", AP via TheNews-Herald.com, December 31, 2016, http://www.news-herald.com/arts-and-entertainment/20161231/2016-year-in-review-lin-manuel-miranda-named-ap-entertainer-of-the-year

11. Andrew Gans, "Lin-Manuel Miranda and Karen Olivo record Audiobook", *Playbill.com*, January 3, 2017, http://www.playbill.com/article/lin-manuel-miranda-and-karen-olivo-record-audiobook

Chapter 7: "What's Comes Next"?

1. Brian Gallagher, "Mary Poppins 2 & Little Mermaid Secrets Shared by Lin-Manuel Miranda", *Movieweb.com*, October 19, 2016, http://movieweb.com/mary-poppins-2-little-mermaid-details-lin-manuel-miranda/

2. Corey Chichizola, "Meet Lin-Manuel Miranda: 9 Fascinating Things to Know About the Hamilton Mastermind", *CinemaBlend*, June 12, 2016, http://www.cinemablend.com/news/1533000/meet-lin-manuel-miranda-9-fascinating-things-to-know-about-the-hamilton-mastermind?story_page=3

3. Julia Brucculieri "Lin-Manuel Miranda Singing Classic Disney Songs on Instagram makes Everything Better", *The Huffington Post*,August 8, 2016, http://www.huffingtonpost.com/entry/lin-manuel-miranda-disney-songs_us_57a89e92e4b021fd987945bd

4. Ibid.

5. Julie Miller, "Update: Disney's *Mary Poppins* Sequel Will Star Emily Blunt and Lin-Manuel Miranda", *VanityFair.com*, February 24, 2016, http://www.

vanityfair.com/hollywood/2016/02/mary-poppins-hamilton-lin-manuel-miranda

6. Ibid

7. Ryan McPhee, "Ben Whishaw Could Join Emily Blunt & Lin-Manuel Miranda for *Mary Poppins Returns*", *Broadway.com*, August 15, 2016, http://www.broadway.com/buzz/185681/ben-whishaw-could-join-emily-blunt-lin-manuel-miranda-for-mary-poppins-returns/

8. Yohana Desta, "Disney Is Lin-Manuel Miranda's Biggest Fan, Taps Him for *Little Mermaid*", *VanityFair.com*, August 16, 2016, http://www.vanityfair.com/hollywood/2016/08/lin-manuel-miranda-little-mermaid

9. Ibid.

10. Noel Holston "The Ultumate Show Biz Coup: PEGOT", *Peabodyawards.com*, http://www.peabodyawards.com/stories/story/the-ultimate-show-biz-coup-pegot

11. Ellen Gamerman, "With Pulitzer Prize, Lin-Manuel Miranda Becomes Leading Contender for MacPEGOT", *The Wall Street Journal*, April 18, 2016, http://blogs.wsj.com/speakeasy/2016/04/18/with-pulitzer-prize-lin-manuel-miranda-becomes-leading-contender-for-macpegot/

12. Fresh Air, "Lin-Manuel Miranda on Disney, Mixtapes, And Why He Won't Try To Top 'Hamilton'", *NPR.org*, January 3, 2017, http://www.npr.org/2017/01/03/507470975/lin-manuel-miranda-

on-disney-mixtapes-and-why-he-wont-try-to-top-hamilton

13. Tracy Browni, "Lin-Manuel Miranda joins 'The Kingkiller Chronicle' film and TV adaptations", *The Los Angeles Times*, November 29, 2016, http://www.latimes.com/entertainment/la-et-entertainment-news-updates-lin-manuel-miranda-joins-the-1480459239-htmlstory.html

14. Ibid.

15. Ibid.

16. Ibid.

17. Ibid.

18. Lin-Manuel Miranda "Stop the Bots From Killing Broadway", *The New York Times*, June 7, 2016, http://www.nytimes.com/2016/06/07/opinion/stop-the-bots-from-killing-broadway.html?_r=0

19. Rebecca Fishbein, "Lin-Manuel Miranda Now Duelling Ticket Bots Instead of Aaron Burr", *Gothamist.com*, August 15, 2016, http://gothamist.com/2016/08/15/lin-manuel_miranda_now_dueling_tick.php

20. Andrea Romano, "Odds of winning 'Hamilton' ticket are bleak, but not as bad as you think", *Mashable.com*, May 26, 2016, http://mashable.com/2016/05/26/odds-of-winning-a-hamilton-ticket/#mKwJkNyh4gq0

21. Forrest Wickman, "The Show is NonStop", *Slate.com*, November 24, 2015, http://www.slate.com/articles/arts/theater/2015/11/ham4ham_lin_manuel_

miranda_and_the_cast_of_hamilton_reward_ticket_
lottery.html

22. Lin-Manuel Miranda "Stop the Bots From Killing
    Broadway", *The New York Times*, June 7, 2016, http://
    www.nytimes.com/2016/06/07/opinion/stop-the-bots-
    from-killing-broadway.html?_r=0

23. Nick Romano, "Lin-Manuel Miranda sings Disney
    tunes for Instagram takeover", *EntertainmentWeekly.
    com*, August 7, 2016, http://ew.com/
    article/2016/08/07/lin-manuel-miranda-sings-disney-
    tunes/

24. Ibid.

25. My Brother, My Brother And Me, March 24, 2014,
    http://mbmbam.libsyn.com/my-brother-my-brother-
    and-me-193-journey-to-the-center-of-the-bear

26. Fresh Air, "Lin-Manuel Miranda on Disney,
    Mixtapes, And Why He Won't Try To Top
    'Hamilton'", *NPR.org*, January 3, 2017, http://www.
    npr.org/2017/01/03/507470975/lin-manuel-miranda-
    on-disney-mixtapes-and-why-he-wont-try-to-top-
    hamilton

27. Gordon Cox, "'Hamilton' Star Lin-Manuel
    Miranda Is Readt for His Next Coup", *Variety*,
    September 27, 2016, http://variety.com/2016/legit/
    features/lin-manuel-miranda-hamilton-next-
    projects-1201870498/

28. Angie Han, "Lin-Manuel Miranda's 'Vivo' Coming
    From Sony Animation", *Shalshfilm.com*, December 14,
    2016, http://www.slashfilm.com/lin-manuel-miranda-
    vivo/

29. Taylor Weatherby, "Lin-Manuel Miranda, Justin Timberlake & More React to Golden Globe Nominations", *Billboard.com*, December 12, 2016, http://www.billboard.com/articles/news/7617708/ golden-globe-nominations-reactions-lin-manuel-miranda-justin-timberlake

30. Gordon Cox, "'Hamilton' Star Lin-Manuel Miranda Is Readt for His Next Coup", *Variety*, September 27, 2016, http://variety.com/2016/legit/ features/lin-manuel-miranda-hamilton-next-projects-1201870498/

31. Ibid.

32. Molly Quinton, "Person of the Year: Lin-Manuel Miranda", *The Daily of the University of Washington*, January 5, 2017, http://www.dailyuw.com/arts_ and_leisure/article_530fa002-d2ef-11e6-8685-8b0558d247db.html

Glossary

alma mater An institution where an individual attended school.

anonymity When an individual is not widely known.

bodega A corner store in New York City. They often sell simple groceries, cleaning supplies, and household items.

collaborators People who work together to create something.

conservatory A school where people study the arts (such as theater, dance, or music) exclusively.

earworms Songs or phrases that get stuck in your head.

freestyle A style of rap in which the person improvises his or her lines.

genre A specific type of music, writing, film, or theater that utilizes many of the same components.

improv A type of theater (most often comedy), in which the actors make up their lines while they are performing.

inspiration The process of being stimulated mentally in order to do, say, or create something.

jingles Short songs, often used in advertising, that are meant to stick in a person's head and promote their cause.

lyrics The words to a song.

masterpiece A spectacular piece of art.

monologue A speech given by one person in a play.

phenomenon An impressive and often unforeseen event that occurs.

physical comedy A style of comedy in which the performer uses his or her own body to make funny things happen.

reboot A reimagining of an earlier piece of work, such as a film or a play.

revolutionize To create something totally new out of something already known.

score The music of a play from start to finish, including the parts that are only instrumental.

sketch A short piece of comedy that is written around an idea reflecting pop culture.

straight plays Plays that have no music.

territory An area of land that belongs to another nation.

ticketbots Computer-driven programs that buy up multiple tickets at a time for sporting events, concerts, theater performances, or anything that requires a ticket. Ticketbots are run by individuals who resell these tickets for much more than they purchased them.

understudy A performer who knows a part in a show. The understudy performs the part if the original cast member cannot.

workshopping A series of performances, readings, and working sessions in which a Broadway musical goes from the page to the stage.

Further Reading

Books

Chernow, Ron, *Alexander Hamilton*. New York, NY: Penguin Books, 2005.

Hudes, Quiara Alegria and Lin-Manuel Miranda, *In the Heights: The Complete Book and Lyrics of the Broadway Musical (Applause Libretto Library)*. New York, NY: Applause Theatre & Cinema Books, 2013.

Kraus, Stephanie, *Game Changers: Lin-Manuel Miranda*. Huntington, CA: Teacher Created Materials, 2016.

Miranda, Lin-Manuel, *Hamilton, Easy Piano*. Milwaukee, WI: Hal Leonard, 2016.

Miranda, Lin-Manuel, *Hamilton: The Revolution*. New York, NY: Grand Central Publishing, 2016.

Miranda, Lin-Manuel, Mark Mancina, and Opetaia Foa'I, *Moana: Music from the Motion Picture Soundtrack*. Milwaukee, WI: Hal Leonard, 2016.

Viertel, Jack, *The Secret Life of the American Musical: How Broadway Shows Are Built*. New York, NY: Sarah Crichton Books (Simon & Schuster), 2016.

Websites

Hamilton: An American Musical

http://www.hamiltonbroadway.com

The official website of the Tony award-winning phenomenon.

Lin-Manuel Miranda

http://www.linmanuel.com

Lin-Manuel Miranda's official website, with links to all his social media platforms, as well as a bio, store, news, and contact info.

@Lin_Manuel on Twitter

https://twitter.com/Lin_Manuel

Read Lin-Manuel's tweets and follow him.

Playbill

http://www.playbill.com

The official site for all things Broadway!

Variety

http://variety.com

The official site of the premier source for entertainment, including film, theater, and music.

Index